THE UNEASY CASE FOR PROGRESSIVE
TAXATION

THE UNEASY CASE
FOR PROGRESSIVE TAXATION

By

Walter J. Blum and Harry Kalven, Jr.

Phoenix Books

THE UNIVERSITY OF CHICAGO PRESS

CHICAGO & LONDON

This book is also available in a clothbound edition from

THE UNIVERSITY OF CHICAGO PRESS

THE UNIVERSITY OF CHICAGO PRESS, CHICAGO & LONDON
The University of Toronto Press, Toronto 5, Canada

PREFACE

IN THE YEAR SINCE THIS ESSAY WAS FIRST PUBLISHED IT CONTINUES to be evident that progressive taxation poses a key policy issue for our society. Every controversy about changes in income tax rates is to some extent a controversy over the principle of progression itself. With the advent of a new national administration which is heavily committed to significant tax reduction as soon as practicable, it is likely that the principle of progression once again will be exposed to public scrutiny. In any event, wide support continues to be found for the oblique attack against progression in the form of the proposed constitutional amendment limiting income tax rates to a maximum of 25 per cent—an arrangement which it has been observed would "in effect eliminate progressive income taxation." This concern with progression has become explicit in the most recent version of the proposed amendment (embodied in House Joint Resolution 103 of the Eighty-third Congress, 1st Session) providing that "the Congress by a vote of three-fourths of all the members of each House may fix a maximum top rate in excess of the 25 per centum, for periods, either successive or otherwise, not exceeding one year each, if such rate so fixed does not exceed the lowest rate . . . by more than fifteen percentage points." It is especially noteworthy that the proposals for directly or indirectly limiting progression are offered as constitutional changes, not as mere changes to the statutory tax law, and thus have as their objective the effectuating of a permanent change in policy.

Two recent popular discussions of the income tax point up the difficulties under which public consideration of the case for progression labors. On the one hand, we find so able a student of taxation as Dean Erwin Griswold of the Harvard Law School, in an article in the *Atlantic Monthly* for August, 1952, casually accepting "ability to pay" as a principal justification for progressive taxation. And, on the other hand, we find a prominent lawyer, Samuel B. Pettingill, in an article on progression in the *American Bar Association Journal* for June, 1953, solemnly telling us that under the Sixteenth Amendment, "one plank of the Communist Manifesto of 1848 has been achieved." There are more perplexities in the case for progression than most of its friends have been willing to consider. But surely progression is by no means so alien to the values of democratic capitalism as many of its critics would have us believe. It has been the hope of the present essay to examine critically the merits of the principle of progression without lapsing into the easy complacency of its friends or resorting to the anxious hyperbole of its critics.

Several recent contributions to the scholarship in this field deserve citation. Simon Kuznets' major study, *Shares of Upper Income Groups in Income and Savings* (National Bureau of Economic Research, 1953) and Dudley Seers's pamphlet, *The Levelling of Incomes since 1938* (Oxford: Blackwell, n.d.), furnish, for the United States and England, respectively, careful efforts to tackle the formidable statistical problem of measuring changes in income distribution at various levels in the society. F. Shehab's book, *Progressive Taxation: A Study in the Development of the Progressive Principle in the British Income Tax* (Oxford: Clarendon Press, 1953) adds substantially to the understanding of the political history of progression.

From the point of view of this essay the most engaging of the new items is Bertrand de Jouvenel's little book, *The Ethics of Redistribution* (Cambridge, 1951). The special merit of De Jouvenel's treatment is that he completely waives any objections to the leveling of incomes resting on incentive grounds and proceeds to consider the issue solely in ethical terms. Particularly arresting is the concluding part of the book. After a sympathetic exploration of the difficulties with redistribution of incomes as an ethical ideal, De Jouvenel makes the striking observation that, "during the whole range of life of commercial society, from the end of the Middle Ages to our day, the wealth of the rich merchant has been resented far more than the pomp of rulers." This leads him to pose as a final challenge the pointed query whether the mass of mankind are not more concerned with who the "unequals" are than with the fact of economic inequality.

The plan of the present essay can be readily summarized. Once the central question has been stated precisely (§§ 1 and 2), the essay turns to a review of the constitutional law about progression (§ 3) and then to a brief survey of the political history of the idea (§ 4). Consideration of the merits of progression begins with an examination of three pervasive objections to it: that it greatly complicates the positive law of taxation; that it is conducive to political irresponsibility; and that it dampens economic incentives (§ 5). After making explicit the general assumption that the burden of the personal income tax is not shifted (§ 6), the remainder of the essay is devoted to a study of the various affirmative arguments for progression.

The first of these to be considered is the most recent and sophisticated justification, that progression aids in maintaining economic stability and a high level of business activity (§ 7). Next treated is the classical argument calling for taxes to be levied in accordance with the benefits received by the taxpayer from government (§ 8).

The essay then turns to a detailed scrutiny of the various and elaborate efforts to justify progression on the hypothesis that money has a declining utility. This segment of the essay begins with the case for progression on the grounds that it equalizes sacrifices among taxpayers (§§ 9 and 10). It then moves to the case for progression in terms of minimizing the aggregate sacrifice of all taxpayers (§ 11). The ultimate premise of all sacrifice theories—that money has a declining utility—is thereafter critically examined (§ 12). Study of sacrifice theory concludes with a review of two variants of sacrifice analysis: that based on the taxpayer's "ability to pay" (§ 13) and that based on normative judgments about the social values of different consumer expenditures accompanying differences in income (§ 14).

The next several sections again form a unit and deal with the perplexities of justifying progression on the ground that it lessens economic inequality. The discussion opens with a series of introductory observations to the effect that progression inevitably operates to reduce economic inequality; that there has been some lack of candor about this fact in our society; and that, once the equalitarian aspects of progression are made explicit, the special topic of progression tends to get lost in the larger issues of economic equality (§ 15). The discussion then proceeds to appraise the advantages and disadvantages of redistribution to the recipients and to the community as a whole (§ 16). It then looks at the ethics of redistribution by considering the claims of the wealthy to the income which it is proposed to take from them via progression (§ 17). The unit is brought to a close by a consideration of the case for redistribution in terms of equality of opportunity, particularly as it affects children (§ 18), and a general summary of the case for progression in terms of lessening economic inequality (§ 19).

The last line of justification for progression is keyed to the exemption of a minimum amount of income from tax. Since such exemptions are almost universally accepted and since they produce a form of progression for taxpayers above the exemption, the implications of the case for exemptions on the case for progression are traced in some detail (§§ 20 and 21).

A final section considers whether any of the preceding analysis of the merits of progression is affected by consideration of how the government spends the tax money which it collects (§ 22).

This essay has had the benefit of the reading and criticism of several colleagues on the law school and economics faculties. We should like in particular to acknowledge our debt to Professor Aaron Director for many kindnesses, including making us uneasy.

W. J. B.

H. K., Jr.

University of Chicago Law School

INTRODUCTION—1963

A DECADE HAS NOW PASSED SINCE THE PUBLICATION OF THIS ESSAY. We are pleased to have the excuse of its republication to return to the perplexities of the case for progressive taxation. The topic has survived the decade almost unchanged. The income tax with high and steeply graduated surtax rates remains a major feature of American life; and, even as we write, general tax reduction is again in the headlines, stirring up debate over the basic policy of progression.

On rereading the essay, we are disposed to leave it stand unchanged. There has been a good deal of writing on the issue in the intervening ten years, adding insight and precision here and there to the analysis. But progression seems to be one of those subjects on which major new lines of thought are not to be expected. Our own views likewise remain largely unchanged. We would still say, "The case for progression, after a long critical look, turns out to be stubborn but uneasy."[1]

I

Some years ago we engaged in a program to gain empirical knowledge relating to the progression question. The University of Chicago Law School had undertaken a series of projects in what was called law and behavioral science in an effort to apply the research techniques of the social sciences to the study of legal problems and institutions. As part of this program, we started to explore the community sense of justice as it related to the tax burden. The key method of inquiry was that of the large-scale public opinion survey, and at the core of the study was the objective of assessing popular attitudes toward progressive taxation.[2] For a variety of reasons the study was never completed, but the experience with it provides a refreshing stimulus to further reflection about progression.

We were determined to probe how deeply the public was committed

---

[1] See text, p. 103 infra.

[2] We examined the problems and the promise of public opinion surveys in Blum & Kalven, The Art of Opinion Research: A Lawyer's Appraisal of an Emerging Science, 24 U. Chi. L. Rev. 1 (1956).

In referring to impressions we gained from the early phases of the empirical study, we risk overstatement. The study was put into the field only in a most preliminary way and on a very small scale, with no effort to utilize proper sampling techniques.

to progression and on what basis. From the start, our social science colleagues had warned that, except in time of actual emergency, no public issue is really salient in popular thought. Nevertheless we were sanguine: the federal income tax was one law with which virtually everyone had direct contact, high surtax rates had been a prominent feature of the law for almost a generation, and, if there was any vitality at all to the notion of a community sense of justice as a foundation for law,[3] it should appear in considering the blunt issue of how the tax burden in fairness ought to be allocated among individuals.

Pilot operations indicated that our expectations were clearly in error. Tax questions generally were of little interest to the public, and among tax questions the issue of distributing the tax burden ranked near the bottom. Even when we had reconciled ourselves to the absence of any conscious opinion and had turned to search for "latent sentiments," our efforts were almost completely frustrated. The precise difficulties are worth emphasizing here. Except for a relatively small elite, the very notion of a *progressive* tax proved to be beyond grasp. By and large people could understand the concept of the wealthy paying more in tax than the less wealthy, but they did not comprehend the idea of the wealthy paying more than a proportionately greater tax than the less wealthy. Proportionate and progressive rate schedules simply were not seen as involving a choice of principles. This same mathematical barrier probably accounted for another difficulty. It is our impression that most people were interested only in the level of their own taxes and not in the ratio of that level to the tax burden on others with different incomes.

In probing as deeply as we could for the reason why the few who did understand the progression principle thought the rich should pay more, we were unable to find anything other than simple, unanalyzed ability-to-pay notions. There was virtually no associating taxes with economic incentives or purchasing power—or with envy or hostility to the rich or with concern over economic inequality.

There was one other clue from the study that seemed rich in political implications. People, it appeared, would distribute a tax increase differently than a tax reduction. They thought it most fair to handle an increase by putting relatively larger burdens on the rich, but, in the case of a reduction, they thought it most fair to give relatively more of the benefit to the less wealthy rather than return to the tax distribution that

[3] The most extensive recent effort to relate public opinion and the community sense of justice to legal rules is Cohen, Robson & Bates, Parental Authority: The Community and the Law (1958). For a critical comment on the study see Kalven, Book Review, 14 Rutgers L. Rev. 843 (1960).

had prevailed before the increase. In any change in total taxes, either up or down, the popular view of fairness would tend to make the rate structure more progressive.

The Uneasy Case was an effort to explore what might be called the intellectual case for progression. In making the empirical tax study, our aim was to lay the results of a public opinion survey alongside the original essay. To the faintest degree, an interesting contrast emerged from the pilot work: the public, unlike a few intellectuals, virtually never thinks of the progressive tax as an instrument for reducing economic inequality. But more basic is the fact that the progression issue is so far beyond the reach of public opinion that it is futile and misleading to talk here of comparing expert opinion and public opinion.

This massive absence of any public opinion, except among the elite, adds a new puzzle to the political history of progression. In the essay we had noted that the intellectual arguments in support of progression all came well after progression had become a political fact.[4] It could be inferred that the intellectuals were following the public rather than leading it and were seeking to find a rational basis for a strong but unarticulated popular sentiment.[5] The sources of the political development, which ten years ago we found to be obscure, now seem to be more mysterious than ever. It is hard to believe that the tiny public sentiment which we were able to unearth could ever have been strong enough to produce the political fact of progression.

2

One of the most notable recent developments on the world scene has been the emergence of the new nations. As the leaders of these countries have turned to the older states for counsel, the economic problems of underdeveloped countries have become widely discussed. High among these problems has been tax policy. The literature on tax policy for underdeveloped countries provides a second novel vantage point for reflecting again on progressive taxation.

Observers generally agree that there are a number of characteristics common to most of the underdeveloped countries.

First, there is an extremely wide discrepancy in wealth and income between a relatively small high income group and a majority of the population whose income borders on subsistence. Second, the high income group is the focus, or more accurately the essence, of whatever political or economic stability exists. This group,

---

[4] See text, pp. 11–14 infra.

[5] For some speculations on the role of the intellectuals on roughly comparable public issues, see Hayek, The Intellectuals and Socialism, 16 U. Chi. L. Rev. 417 (1949).

tracing its wealth and position to large landholdings, tends to dominate the social, political, and economic structures of the nation. Finally, there is an ardent desire to be considered a modern progressive nation with political autonomy.[6]

Under these conditions, the development of tax policy is caught in a sharp cross fire. On the one side there is a strong need to preserve economic incentives and not to alienate the economic elite who are a key source of stability. On the other side there is a strong desire to utilize sharply progressive taxes.

Two sources of this momentum toward progression are of special interest. There is the wish to emulate what is considered to be the moral style of advanced countries, and a distinctly progressive tax structure is viewed as a mark of a civilized country. As one observer has put it: "Progressive income taxation is desired simply because it is regarded as one of the symbols of modern government."[7] There is, as another source, an emphasis the bluntness of which may be startling to those conditioned to the tradition of American political discussion. Official statements of policy in underdeveloped countries are explicitly phrased in terms of redistributing wealth or income. It is made clear that the attraction of progression for these countries is that it will mitigate economic inequalities. An Indian Commission reporting on tax policy a few years back listed as the first main criterion of a tax system: ". . . the incidence of a tax system and its suitability for reducing inequality of income and wealth, viz., the distribution of the burden of taxation and its redistributive effects and possibilities."[8] The commission went on to observe:

We can no longer afford to leave the problem of equality to the automatic functioning of economic and social forces. . . . The demand that the instrument of taxation should be used as a means of bringing about a redistribution of income, more in consonance with social justice, cannot be kept in abeyance.[9]

But these spokesmen are equally explicit in recognizing the conflict between objectives. Nowhere are the tensions between the equalitarian aspirations and the disincentive effects of progression seen more vividly. The variety of responses to this conflict could almost have been predicted. At one extreme is the view that progression is compatible only with a mature economy; in the words of one observer, "extensive reliance on income taxes or other ability to pay measures is a social and economic

---

[6] Shirley, Income Taxes for Lesser Developed Nations? 12 Nat'l Tax J. 265 (1959).

[7] Ibid.

[8] Report of the Taxation Enquiry Commission (Dep't of Economic Affairs, Gov't of India), c. VIII, ¶5 (1953–54).

[9] Ibid.

luxury which the lesser developed nations of the world cannot yet afford."[10] The advice which follows is to separate the political and economic
objectives by offering little more than lip service to progression so as to
satisfy the required political rhetoric. At the opposite pole is the conclusion of a United Nations Technical Assistance Report: "Redistributive
finance appears to offer greater gains and involve less cost to underdeveloped than to developed economies."[11] This view proceeds not only
from a willingness to have the government perform the main role in
capital formation but also from the premise that, given the structure of
underdeveloped economies, the major disincentives will fall on *rentiers*
rather than on entrepreneurs. In between these extremes is the hopeful
position voiced by the Indian Commission: "Ways and means, therefore,
must be devised to insure simultaneous progress in both directions, viz.,
of greater production and of better distribution."[12] The expectation
apparently is that it will be possible to build into a progressive tax structure a set of exceptions and qualifications which will maintain the necessary incentives for specific economic functions without destroying its
redistributive potential.[13]

Thus, although the relevant conditions in underdeveloped countries
would seem to be dramatically different from circumstances in the
United States, the progression issue, when transplanted, is no less uneasy.
But the grossness of the inequalities of wealth and income and the depth
of poverty in those countries cause a marked difference in the prevailing
rhetoric.[14]

[10] Shirley, supra note 6, at 269.

[11] U.N. Technical Assistance Administration, Taxes and Fiscal Policy in Underdeveloped
Countries 18 (1954).

[12] Report of the Taxation Enquiry Commission, op. cit. supra note 8.

[13] On the problem of tailoring a tax system to the needs of an underdeveloped country, see
Goode, Taxation of Saving and Consumption in Underdeveloped Countries, 14 Nat'l Tax J.
305 (1961).

[14] In discussions of economic aspects of tax policy in the United States, the progression
issue continues to appear with some frequency. There have been numerous assertions to the
effect that a more progressive tax structure, as compared to a less progressive one yielding the
same amount of tax revenue, would contribute significantly to bringing about or maintaining
a high level of employment of resources. Although this position sometimes seems to be a
rationalization for a deeper conviction that heavier taxes should be placed upon the wealthy
and lighter taxes on the less wealthy, it also seems to have genuine adherents. It appears to
rest on the propositions that the budget of the federal government should be in balance (or
at a minimum deficit) over some period of time; that a dollar of tax taken from the less wealthy
will reduce total private demand more than a dollar taken from the rich, because the latter
generally save a larger percentage of their incomes than the former; and that there is a tendency for investment demands to fall short of savings at the level of income at full employment.
Reasoning from these propositions, however, is treacherous. The government can alter total
demand by means outside the tax system through monetary operations. Moreover, for the

3

Ten years ago we were puzzled as to why Henry Simons' bluntness
had not had more impact on the tone of discussions in the United States.
Writing in the late thirties, he exasperatedly asserted that the whole
superstructure of sacrifice and ability-to-pay theorizing was simply nonsense and that the case for progression was no more and no less than the
case for mitigating "unlovely" economic inequality.[15] One then would
have thought that the cat had been let out of the bag forever and would
have predicted that discussion of progression would never be the same
after this outburst of candor.

On reviewing the recent literature on the redistributive aspects of
progression, we note some interesting changes in emphasis, but on the
whole the approach to redistribution by those favoring progression[16] is
still curious. The most obvious change is the diminished appetite for
justifying progression on the basis of sacrifice analysis and its many
subtleties.[17] What is particularly noteworthy is that in virtually sur-

---

type of analysis being offered, there is no need to stay within the premise that the budget
must remain in balance (or at a minimum deficit); it is at least conceivable that, under some
circumstances, total demand can be augmented by running a deficit (or a larger deficit) for a
limited period. Further, we know too little about savings patterns and propensities to assume
that a move to decrease the after-tax income of the wealthy and to increase the after-tax
income of the less wealthy by the same amount would change the overall ratio of savings to
income. See Stein, Stimulation of Consumption or Investment through Tax Policy, in Joint
Committee on the Economic Report, in 84th Cong. 1st Sess., Federal Tax Policy for Economic
Growth and Stability 245 (Nov. 9, 1955). See also Samuelson, The New Look in Tax and Fiscal
Policy, id. at 233, 234, who concludes: "A community can have full employment, and at the
same time have the rate of capital formation it wants, and can accomplish all this compatibly
with the degree of income-redistributing taxation it ethically desires." Compare Rolph,
Equity Versus Efficiency in Federal Tax Policy, 40 Am. Econ. Rev. 394 (1950).

There is recent evidence that the savings-income ratio in our society has been fairly constant throughout a very wide range of incomes over a long time. Friedman, A Theory of the
Consumption Function (1957). If this proposition turns out to be generally correct, it would
undermine the argument that progressive taxation impairs economic growth by reducing
aggregate savings. It would also pose a problem for those who seek to step up the rate of our
economic growth. If over time the propensity to save is fairly constant among various income
levels, a program to augment growth would seem to require that increased attention be paid
to incentives and to the "investment climate." As to the impact of progression on incentives,
see text, pp. 21–28 infra.

[15] The Simons remark is quoted in the essay at 72 infra; the original passage is found in
Simons, Personal Income Taxation 18–19 (1938).

[16] The conservative writers, it is not surprising, have been much more direct in dealing with
redistribution. See especially three statements by F. A. Hayek: The Constitution of Liberty
306–23 (1960); The Case against Progressive Income Taxes, The Freeman, Dec. 28, 1953, p.
229; Progressive Taxation Reconsidered, in On Freedom and Free Enterprise 265 (1956).

Taxation apart, attention continues to be paid to the subject of economic inequality itself.
Of particular interest are Oliver, A Critique of Socioeconomic Goals (1954); Lampman, Recent
Thoughts on Equalitarianism, 71 Q. J. Econ. 234 (1957).

[17] As late as March 10, 1963, it appeared that sacrifice theory was not without distinguished
support. In answer to the question, posed by a resident of Lewiston, Utah, "What do the great

rendering sacrifice analysis, with its postulate of declining marginal
utility of money, the defenders of progression have not followed the path
of Simons. Instead, they are willing to acknowledge redistribution as
relevant but are unwilling to rest the case for progression on it. Typical
of such contemporary commentators is Roy Blough.[18] After saying that
sacrifice, faculty, and even benefit theories "point to progression, but only
in a rather moderate degree," he argues that the current tax rates "involve also at least a degree of skepticism that the distribution of income
is demonstrably the best one." And having so modestly indorsed the
equalitarian rationale for progression, he adds the further qualification
that the "attitude that has chiefly been involved" is not that of "deliberately using tax and expenditure measures to reduce the incomes of
people because these are deemed to be too high" but rather that of
"looking around for the best place to impose taxes that have to be levied
on someone."

Another recent commentator, Louis Eisenstein, is likewise chary in
dealing with progression and economic equality.[19] He moves rapidly
through three positions. Initially, he sees as a special weakness of sacrifice
or ability-to-pay theories that their claim to neutrality is an illusion since
in fact taxes have effects on the distribution of wealth and income. Accordingly, he finds inescapable the proposition of Simons that "it is only
sensible to face the question as to what kinds of effects are desirable."[20]
A few pages later, however, he tells us that "though we still have progression, it is no longer prudent to say in so many words that the primary
purpose of the graduated rates is to diminish the economic differences
that characterize our economy."[21] Next, he asserts that whether prudent
or not there would be no point in confronting the equality question
directly inasmuch as there is no way of answering the question, "If the
rates are to mitigate inequalities of wealth, how drastic should they be
in pursuit of this objective?"[22] And he adds, "Everyone who meditates
on such problems will respond in the light of his own views on equality."[23]

A different resolution of the equality issue is put forward by Harold

---

thinkers have to say about the purpose and limit of taxation that a country imposes upon its
citizens?" Mortimer J. Adler, the director of the Philosophical Institute, replied in part:
"The argument for graduated tax rates is that they equalize the sacrifice involved. A man
earning $4,000 a year is far more grievously hit by a tax of 10 per cent than a man earning
$40,000 a year." Chicago Sun-Times, March 10, 1963, § 2, p. 13.

[18] Blough, Basic Tax Issues, in The History and Philosophy of Taxation 21 (1955).

[19] Eisenstein, The Ideologies of Taxation 16–33 (1961). For a critical review see Blum,
Book Review, 56 Nw. U. L. Rev. 692 (1961).

[20] Eisenstein, op. cit. supra note 19, at 26.   [22] Id., at 32.

[21] Id., at 31.   [23] Ibid.

Groves.[24] In his words, he wishes to find a position which affords "a detour around the futile snarls of the classical case" of sacrifice theory and "the pure value judgments of the Simons-Taussig school." He rejects sacrifice theory because it does not persuade and he rejects the equalitarian value judgment because it is "debate closing." As a solution, following the line of argument developed by Elmer Fagan,[25] he urges placing the case on the total effects of progression. In setting tax policy, he would have us interested in

what progressive taxation will do to serve or disserve such widely accepted national objectives as an increase in per capita real income, minimum economic fluctuations, a workable tax system producing adequate revenue, political stability under representative government, international independence or security, elimination of extreme want, and perhaps mitigation of social disorders, such as crime, divorce, mental illness and the like.[26]

Tax alternatives, in short, should be weighed "not in terms of the personal but rather the social significance of income."[27] On this view, the distribution of income becomes only one among many factors to be considered in appraising progression; in Groves's phrase, it is treated "as an intermediate means rather than an end."[28]

The positions taken by Blough, Eisenstein, and Groves, although quite distinct from each other,[29] leave a common impression. The whole issue of redistribution is muted and is handled with gentility. Even with the props of sacrifice theory substantially removed, there is still a strong pull away from resting the case for progression squarely on doing something about economic inequalities. This, however, seems not so much due now to a default in candor. Rather it appears to arise from two other sources. First, there is a sense of despair over arguing the case for progression on grounds of a subjective judgment about what degree of inequality is disturbing in our society. Second, there is a disinclination to

---

[24] Groves, Toward a Social Theory of Taxation, 9 Nat'l Tax J. 27 (1956).

[25] See text, p. 75, n. 185 infra.

[26] Groves, op. cit. supra note 24, at 31.   [27] Id., at 34.

[28] Id., at 31.
More recently Groves, in applying his general approach, has suggested that the case for progression at the top of the income scale might be rested on different grounds than in the lower ranges. At the top, progression might be justified as a matter of checking and dispersing power, while in the lower ranges it might be justified in terms of welfare and conserving human resources. It is expected that this view will be developed in more detail by Groves in a background paper prepared for a conference on The Tax Treatment of the Family, under the auspices of The Brookings Institution as part of its Studies of Government Finance program.

[29] For a summary of some other fairly recent views on the subject, see Paul, Taxation in the United States 731–64 (1954).

treat economic inequality in contemporary America as a very serious social problem. Eisenstein has recently put his finger on the point: "The usual liberal approach today is that if we can promote economic growth, if we can have a larger pie, all segments of society will necessarily have larger shares of that pie and we won't have to worry about redistribution of income anymore."[30] This strikes us as a shrewd insight into the changing scene, and one which has been noted by others.[31] But while it may explain why current writing does not re-echo the intensity of Simons, it more than ever leaves the intellectual case for progression in the obscurantist's vein.

4

It is important that discussion of progressive taxation not be confused with the policy of selecting income as a tax base. Whatever uneasiness exists over the first policy issue does not carry over to the second. It is precisely on the issue of the proper tax base that the criterion of ability to pay is powerful. There is a high level of agreement that, in an advanced economy, income is a superior measure of the ability to pay taxes.[32] The essay therefore was confined pretty strictly to a consideration of progression in an income tax alone.

Admittedly, there is a certain hiatus in theorizing about progressive taxation if the analysis does not look to wealth as well as to income. But the emendation is relatively small. As a practical matter, the income tax is overwhelmingly a more dominant tax than the wealth-transfer taxes in our society—for 1962 the federal government collected about fifty billion dollars under the individual income tax as against about two billion under the estate and gift taxes. Further, while there are some differences in the rationale for progression under an income tax and under a wealth-transfer tax, it is improbable that anyone who favored progressive income taxes would balk at progressive transfer taxes.[33] Insofar as we are interested in pursuing the merits of progressive taxation, the income tax then is the proper forum for the main inquiry.

[30] Eisenstein, Cahn, Arnold & McDonald, A Discussion of "The Ideologies of Taxation," 18 Tax L. Rev. 1, 4 (1962).

[31] "However, few things are more evident in modern social history than the decline of interest in inequality as an economic issue. This has been especially true in the United States." Galbraith, The Affluent Society 82 (1958).

[32] But see Kaldor, An Expenditure Tax (1955) and his comment, The Reform of Personal Taxation, 6 Can. Tax J. 249 (1958).

[33] The converse position has a different force: it can be argued that the rationale for progression is persuasive in the case of wealth-transfer taxes but not in the case of income or expenditure taxes. See text, p. 87, n. 213 infra.

However, in considering the redistributive objectives of a progressive income tax, a fruitful question can arise as to relationship of the income tax to wealth-transfer taxes. If the income tax alone is progressive, the effect is to make more rigid certain economic inequalities. The income tax can do nothing to mitigate existing inequalities in wealth, and, moreover, it retards the accumulation of new fortunes. The progressive income tax alone, no matter how steep the progression, tends to preserve and magnify the advantages of inherited wealth.

Conversely, a progressive transfer tax alone without a progressive income tax could do little by way of redistribution in our society. As one writer, Henry M. Oliver, Jr., has phrased it: "Income taxes . . . offer much greater opportunities for redistribution than do inheritance taxes, since the total amount of income in any one year is a sizeable percentage of the total estimated value of wealth, whereas only a small percentage of wealth annually changes hands through inheritance."[34]

For the person who wishes to redress economic inequalities, it appears that both a progressive wealth-transfer tax and a progressive income tax are congenial tools. But a combination of steeply progressive transfer and income taxes might have some untoward side effects in dampening economic incentives and in aggravating the problem of liquidating large holdings under the transfer tax.[35] At some levels of tax, the equalitarian may be faced with the interesting choice whether wealth or income inequalities are the more disturbing. It would seem that over the centuries disparities in wealth have been unsettling; today one could make out a strong case that in our society income disparities have come to dominate whatever dissatisfaction is felt.

5

Progression has often been challenged as a politically irresponsible measure. The classic argument against it on this ground is that the majority is permitted to vote a rate of tax for the minority to which the

[34] Oliver, op. cit. supra note 16, at 80.

[35] "If government placed very steep taxes on both medium-high incomes and medium-high inheritances, it would derive much less revenue from the latter than might seem reasonable at first glance. A few decades of such taxes would mean the virtual disappearance of private demand at 'reasonably high' prices for the properties represented by the taxed estates. The government would thus have the choice of collecting tax revenues represented by diminished sales values, of leasing the estates to private tenants, or of operating the estates as public enterprises. . . . To the extent that sale at depressed prices was the alternative chosen, a curious type of income redistribution would take place. Persons with moderate holdings of liquid assets or of fairly good credit ratings could acquire properties previously thought to represent much higher values, but revenues available for state benefits of a more clearly equalitarian nature would represent a sum much smaller than the total volume of leveling downward achieved." Id., at 96–97.

majority itself is not subject. When the redistributive aspects are made explicit, the majority appears to be invited to vote on the extent to which it wishes to reduce the economic inequalities between itself and a richer minority. The thrust of this observation is most powerful when progressive taxes are contrasted with proportionate taxes—under which the majority is automatically subject to whatever tax rate it has selected. It loses considerable power, however, when progressive taxation is compared with any number of other instances of lawmaking by majority vote. And no matter what the political theory would predict, in practice the progressive rates have somehow not reflected so naked an exercise of sheer majority power.[36]

Other aspects of the political process of tax-rate legislation are attracting increased attention in recent years, especially as tax reduction becomes a national issue. Changes in graduated rates often seem to involve the breaking of an implicit promise. It has been the history of surtaxes that they are imposed or raised as a revenue "necessity" over a short-run emergency but that they stay on the scene long after the emergency has passed. As Lionel Robbins has observed about upper rates of surtax in England: "They were brought into existence at a time of crisis when they did not seem—and indeed were not—inappropriate to the needs of the situation. Now that the crisis has passed, they have continued to exist because those who rule over us have been afraid to challenge the purely demagogic arguments by which they are usually supported."[37] Some observers, like F. A. Hayek, have even doubted that in recent emergencies the revenue goals could have been satisfied only through higher surtaxes. "It would probably be true," argues Hayek, ". . . to say that the illusion that by means of progressive taxation the burden can be shifted substantially onto the shoulders of the wealthy has been the chief reason why taxation has increased as fast as it has done, and that, under the influence of this illusion, the masses have come to accept a much heavier load than they would have done otherwise."[38]

The political process is challenged here because the rates are unlikely

---

[36] There are complications in reading the historical record on this point. F. A. Hayek, for example, states flatly that "all the assurances that progression will remain moderate have proved false and . . . its development has gone far beyond the most pessimistic prognostications of its opponents. . . ." Hayek, The Constitution of Liberty 213 (1960). On the other hand, maximum rates of surtax in England, Canada, and the United States have been substantially reduced at times during the period 1900–1955. See First National City Bank Monthly Letter, June, 1955, p. 71. The steepness of surtax rates should not be confused with the general level of taxation.

[37] Robbins, Notes on Public Finance, Lloyds Bank Rev., Oct. 1955, p. 1.

[38] Hayek, The Constitution of Liberty 311 (1950).

to come down by the same route that they went up.[39] At the time of an emergency which brings about a tax increase, it appears that a sudden new burden can be more easily borne by the rich, thus suggesting that the tax system be made more progressive in the upper-income ranges. When tax reduction is in the air, it appears that the less rich are more deserving of the reduction, thus suggesting that the system should not return to the tax pattern which prevailed before the increase brought on by the emergency. It is almost as though tax reduction is viewed, not as the erasing of a prior tax burden, but as an independent distribution of a "bonus" by the government. Neutrality in tax reduction, although there are some technical difficulties with that concept,[40] would in a simple fashion often require that higher-bracket taxpayers benefit from the tax cut substantially more than those in lower brackets. But this symmetry is not likely to persuade the popular mind.

The hardiness of high progressive surtaxes perhaps is also to be accounted for by other factors. There is a basic rhetorical awkwardness in arguing that high surtaxes should be reduced: to argue for less progressivity is tantamount to arguing for increasing the prevailing degree of economic inequality after taxes. Moreover, progressive rates tend to set their own precedent. The prevailing rates appear to look more equitable and acceptable the longer they have been around.

All these considerations deepen the sense in which progression might be said to be politically irresponsible. It is a legal measure which is peculiarly resistant to sober reconsideration through the political process.

Another characteristic of highly progressive tax rates can be viewed either as exhibiting another species of political irresponsibility or simply as amusing *Realpolitik*. There has always been, both here and in other economically advanced societies, a large degree of official fraud in sponsoring a popular impression as to the amount of actual progressivity in the tax system. High surtax rates have invariably been accompanied by big holes in the tax base, so that the effective rates for most taxpayers

[39] Assistant Secretary of the Treasury, Stanley Surrey, in discussing reactions to the Kennedy administration's current proposal to cut income taxes drastically, recently made the following bemused comment: "High-income taxpayers look at the larger percentage reductions in tax liability going to low- or middle-income taxpayers and feel that those groups are getting too much. . . . Low- and middle-income taxpayers look at the larger dollar reductions and the larger percentage increases in after-tax incomes going to high-income groups, and feel that the upper-income taxpayers are getting too much." Speech before the Union League Club of Chicago, March 18, 1963.

[40] Neutrality in tax reduction in this sense would require that the degree of progressivity be the same before and after the reduction. The key technical difficulty is in locating a criterion for comparing the progressivity of two different sets of rates. See Musgrave & Thin, Income Tax Progression, 56 J. Pol. Econ. 498 (1948).

are totally obscure and undoubtedly far below the published schedule of rates. If one, in the vein of Thurman Arnold, wants to find amusement in the folklore of American politics, this time-honored formula of high surtax rates and big loopholes furnishes a delightful illustration. The classic objection about the political irresponsibility of majority vote seems almost to be turned upside down. Instead of the majority voting high taxes on the minority, the minority seems to have beguiled the majority into thinking that this has actually happened.[41]

Many observers, however, are not amused. They see the formula as handicapping responsible political judgment. It is widely recognized that the present effective rates of income tax are capricious and inequitable because not every taxpayer with the same income is in an equally good position to exploit the gaps in the tax base. It can well be argued that the economic inequalities that thus emerge within our tax system are more disturbing than those that the progressive rates, on any view, were meant to redress. A considered judgment about how progressive the rates should be is virtually impossible because of the confusion between real and nominal progressivity. And the whole process is economically wasteful to boot. As Milton Friedman has argued:

> If present rates were made fully effective, the effect on incentives and the like might well be so serious as to cause a radical loss in the productivity of the society. Tax avoidance may therefore have been essential for economic well-being. If so, the gain has been bought at the cost of a great waste of resources and of the introduction of widespread inequity. A much lower set of nominal rates, plus a more comprehensive base, through more equal taxation of all sources of income could be both more progressive in average incidence, more equitable in detail, and less wasteful of resources.[42]

6

Since publication of the essay, we have occasionally come upon a reader who puts the following challenge: Is not your assessment of the case for

[41] See Blum, Tax Lawyers and Tax Policy, Taxes, March 1961, p. 247.

[42] Friedman, Capitalism and Freedom 173 (1962). See also papers on the economic impact of expansion and contraction of the tax base, in Joint Committee on the Economic Report, 84th Cong. 1st Sess., Federal Tax Policy for Economic Growth and Stability (Nov. 9, 1955).

The problem of equity posed by the combination of an uneven tax base and progressive rates is sometimes described as weighing vertical fairness (that is, fairness as between persons with different levels of economic income) and horizontal fairness (that is, fairness as between persons with the same amount of economic income but otherwise differently situated). Every omission from the tax base tends to increase the tension between the two comparisons. It should be noted, however, that, even if the tax base were virtually all-inclusive, a progressive rate structure would nevertheless produce such tensions; it is not obvious whether the proper taxable unit is the individual, the marital couple, the household, or some other grouping. To a lesser extent these tensions also arise where there is disagreement whether earned and unearned income is to be treated alike under the progressive rates. See text, pp. 14–19 infra.

xxii   INTRODUCTION

progressive taxation incomplete in that you failed to consider how uneasy
the case for proportionate taxation may also be? In brief, is not the real
choice a choice between two uneasinesses?

Such a challenge serves to raise the pertinent question whether proportion can "win" only by default or whether there is an affirmative case
for a proportionate tax system.[43] It is true that the essay did not, in so
many words, examine independently the case for proportion. However,
on closer analysis, it will be seen that the two sections of the essay on
the degressive tax model are much in point.[44]

In our thinking, the significant comparison is not between a system
with a simple flat rate of tax and one with graduated rates. The significant
choice is between two forms of progression. This paradox arises because
we believe that a general exemption for those at the bottom of the income
scale is today both inescapable and desirable; and a general exemption
coupled with a flat rate of tax will produce, as a matter of mathematics,
a set of progressive effective rates of tax.[45] The choice therefore is between
progression in this form—called "degression"—and progression in the
form of graduated marginal rates. On this view, the affirmative case for
proportion reduces to the case for degressive taxation.

Degression usually has been considered only in the context of a modest
general exemption, making the resulting progression seem an incidental
and unimportant by-product. Toward the end of the essay, we speculated
on the possibilities of raising the level of a general exemption enough to
yield a substantial degree of progression. On a rereading, we have little
to add to our earlier discussion of the matter. But we would note three
impressions. First, to an astonishing degree, few of the ideological under-
pinnings used to justify progressive taxation—the scrutiny of which was

[43] To a considerable extent, it is true that the alleged virtues of proportion are simply the
contraries of the alleged weaknesses of progression. See text, especially pp. 94–98 infra.

[44] Text, pp. 90–100 infra.

[45] This point is somewhat overstated. Progression is automatically obtained from an exemption only if the exemption is also granted to those above the exemption level; the degressive
tax pattern results only if the same dollar exemption is granted to all taxpayers regardless of
income. It is of course possible to grant an exemption on other terms. That in fact is done
today in a number of income tax systems, but in the United States general exemptions have
been of the across-the-board type. See text, pp. 91–93 infra.

Exemptions and their consequences are analyzed thoroughly in Levy, Income Tax Exemptions (1960). Four types of exemption phenomena are distinguished: (1) a *continuing* exemption, which is an exemption of a constant amount at all income levels; (2) an *initial* exemption,
which provides an exclusion from the tax base of a minimum income for those whose incomes
do not exceed that minimum; (3) a *vanishing* exemption, which excludes an initial amount of
income and is so arranged that it disappears gradually with mounting income until at some
income level it disappears completely; and (4) a tax credit, which provides a constant amount
of tax saving at all levels of income.

the main business of the essay—are in any way relevant to progression arrived at through degression. Second, in contrast to graduated rates which seem to reflect a concern over the inequalities of income between the middle- and upper-income groups, degression strikingly focuses attention on the inequality between the lowest income groups and all others —that is to say, on the problem of poverty.[46] Third, the degressive model has the impressive attraction of avoiding the excesses of high surtaxes and at the same time preserving the humane concerns of progression—indeed, it would appear to be the almost ideal solution for the uneasy case.[47]

But in the foreseeable future it is unlikely that the history of the federal income tax will repeat itself and return to the degressive pattern.[48] The difficulty, of course, is that, given the heavy national revenue demands on the income tax, it is impractical as a sheer revenue matter to raise the exemption level enough to introduce a significant degree of progression into the system. The loss of revenue through increasing the general exemption would invite a relatively heavy flat rate of tax.[49] The ironic consequence is that we would be giving substantial tax reduction both to upper incomes, through eliminating surtaxes, and to lower incomes, through raising the general exemption, while simultaneously adding to the tax burden of those in the middle, via the heavy flat rate.

Thus, the momentary promise of the degressive alternative is undermined by revenue needs and political realities; and the case for progressive taxation once more turns out to be "stubborn but uneasy."

W. J. B.
H. K., JR.

CHICAGO
March 1963

[46] There is today an emergence of concern over what has been called poverty in an affluent society. See Harrington, The Other America (1963), and MacDonald, Book Review, The New Yorker, Jan. 19, 1963, p. 82.

[47] More than a faint suggestion of this approach is to be found in Hayek's proposal to derive the schedule of tax rates by first fixing the top marginal rate of tax and making it applicable to the majority of taxpayers. Hayek, The Constitution of Liberty 322–23 (1960).

[48] The point is, of course, that the income tax of 1894, which was held to be unconstitutional on other grounds, had a flat rate of 2% and a general exemption of $4,000. See text, p. 7 infra.

[49] Another method of recapturing the lost revenue would be to broaden the tax base substantially by eliminating various deductions, taxing income items now excluded, and applying the ordinary rate to all forms of taxable income.

THE UNEASY CASE FOR PROGRESSIVE
TAXATION

I

PROGRESSIVE TAXATION IS NOW REGARDED AS ONE OF THE CENTRAL
ideas of modern democratic capitalism and is widely accepted as a secure
policy commitment which does not require serious examination. The
single topic of this essay is the extent to which progressive taxation can
be justified.

It may seem something of a luxury to indulge in an extensive investiga-
tion of this question at the present time. There are, to be sure, some indica-
tions that the subject is newsworthy. The State of Illinois is currently considering an amendment to its constitution to permit the enactment of a
state income tax. While there is considerable support for the adoption of
an income tax, there is widespread insistence that the amendment contain
an explicit prohibition against a progressive income tax.[1] On the national
scene attention is finally being paid to the proposal to amend the Constitution to limit the rates of federal income taxes by imposing a ceiling of
twenty-five per cent.[2] It is clear that the amendment has as one of its prin-

[1] Both Houses of the Illinois legislature have approved a resolution calling for submitting
to the electorate in November 1952 a proposal to amend various sections of the revenue article
of the Illinois Constitution. Proposed new Section 2 provides: "The General Assembly may
levy or authorize the levy of such other kinds of taxes as it may deem necessary, which shall
be uniform upon the same class of subjects within the territorial limits of the authority
levying the tax, but shall not levy or authorize the levy of a graduated income tax." 7th
General Assembly, Illinois, House Joint Resolution 40 (1951). The wording of the amendment
may conceal a serious ambiguity as to whether the prohibition extends to the kind of progression that results from granting an exemption. See text, section 20 infra. The proposed
amendment was discussed at the University of Chicago Law School Conference on Illinois
Constitutional Amendments, Evening Session, May 15, 1951.

[2] See H.J. Res. 323, 82d Cong. 1st Sess. (1951); H.J. Res. 268, 82d Cong. 1st Sess. (1951);
S.J. Res. 108, 82d Cong. 1st Sess. (1951). The proposed amendment is subjected to appropriate

cipal purposes the curtailing of progression, at least during periods of peace. On the international level the progression issue has put in an appearance in the discussions of how the costs of maintaining a common military organization are to be apportioned among the member nations of the North Atlantic Treaty Organization. The argument is repeatedly being advanced that the progressive principle in the tax systems of the individual countries offers strong precedent for adapting the principle to this new situation.[3] Apart from these current developments, it is always true that every adjustment of federal tax rates necessarily calls into active question the principle of progression. Any change in the rates either reaffirms the existing degree of progression or alters it. The basic considerations advanced in every controversy about rate changes echo the arguments for and against the principle of progression itself.[4]

These current matters, however, are not the motivating force for this essay. It arises out of an attempt to satisfy our curiosity. Like most people today we found the notion of progression immediately congenial. Upon early analysis the notion retained its attractiveness, but our curiosity as to the source of its appeal increased. The somewhat paradoxical character we detected in the topic is suggested by certain aspects of its literature. A surprising number of serious writers note that progression seems to be instinctively· correct, although they then go on to explore it on rational grounds. More striking is the fact that the most devastating critics of the defenses for progression are almost invariably its friends. It is close to the truth to say that only those who ultimately favor progression on some ground have been its effective critics on other grounds.[5] It is as though

---

scrutiny in 29 Taxes (July 1951). If additional literature on the subject is desired, it can be obtained from the Committee for Constitutional Government, 205 East 42d St., New York 17, N.Y.

[3] "Now this principle [of proportion] may be fair. If so, we must not shirk the obvious implications; and it is certain that some countries of continental Europe are not pulling their weight. But in fact the full proportional principle is not in line with modern ideas about the equity of tax burdens. All civilized countries now operate on the progressive and not on the proportionate principle, namely, the principle that persons with a higher real income should contribute a larger proportion of their income in taxation. It would, on this principle, be fair that the United States, with its higher real income per head, should contribute a higher proportion of its national income to the common defence. Indeed, it is inevitable that the progressive principle should be adopted. But if it is adopted, it does, of course, greatly complicate the problem of equitable burden-sharing." Mead, Some Economic Problems of Atlantic Union Rearmament, Lloyds Bank Rev. 35, 40 (Oct. 1951).

[4] See Blough, The Argument Phase of Taxpayer Politics, 17 Univ. Chi. L. Rev. 604 (1950).

[5] Sufficient evidence for this point may be found in the writings of Seligman, Edgeworth, Chapman, Fagan and Simons which are discussed in some detail in the course of the essay. This is not to deny that there are some competent critics who in the end rejected progression, such as Adams and Bastable.

those who have most clearly detected the weaknesses of various lines of analysis previously offered to support progression were under a compulsion to find some new way to justify it rather than give it up. The hunch that there must be some basis on which an idea as initially attractive as progression can be justified is stubborn indeed.

2

It is probable that many do not reach the issues of progression because they tend to regard as decisive the fact that the rich pay more in taxes than the poor. But this is an attribute of both proportionate and progressive taxes and overlooks the real difference between the two. A proportionate tax, for example on income, is one which taxes each dollar of income at the same rate regardless of the total income of the taxpayer; under it a taxpayer with ten times the total income of another would pay ten times as much tax. A progressive tax on income is one whose rate increases as the income of the taxpayer increases; under it a taxpayer with ten times the total income of another would pay something more than ten times as much tax.

There is another basic rate pattern for a tax. The rate of tax, again using a tax on income as an illustration, may be graduated downward with income and thus be regressive; under this pattern a man with ten times the income of another would pay something less than ten times as much tax. It is so clear no one today favors any tax because it is regressive that the term itself has become colored. Since a regressive tax on income is not a serious alternative the question of this essay can be narrowed and restated: On what grounds is a progressive tax on income to be preferred to a proportionate tax on income?

The question requires further qualification. It assumes that the rate of the tax is being measured against income. Income is not the only possible base against which to classify rate patterns; either capital or expenditures could be used.[6] The income base, however, appears to offer the best framework for analysis of the case for progression, and therefore discussion will be focussed on it, although from time to time reference will be made to wealth as a base.

[6] Not every tax base would be equally meaningful for progression; thus a "progressive" tax on the consumption of milk would almost certainly be regressive as measured by income or wealth. "Progressive taxes may be divided into two general types: one type of tax is based on a flow of money or goods and services during a given period of time, the other on a stock of capital or goods belonging to a taxpayer at a given point in time. The principal exemplars of the 'flow' type of tax are the income tax and the spendings tax; the 'stock of goods' type of tax includes property taxes, net worth taxes, capital levies, and succession taxes." Vickrey, Agenda for Progressive Taxation 4 (1947).

One thing more is required to state the question precisely. Progression can refer either to progression in the marginal rates of tax or progression in the effective rates of tax.[7] Marginal rates graduated upwards always produce progressive effective rates, but it is possible to obtain progressive effective rates without having progressive marginal rates. Under a single rate of tax the granting of an exemption to all taxpayers results in a progression of effective rates. Such progression comes about because the taxpayers have a progressively larger fraction of their incomes subject to tax once they are over the exemption level. The effective rates on total income vary from a zero rate at the point of the exemption to a rate approaching, but never quite reaching, the single flat rate of tax. This is easily seen by considering the combination of a $1,000 exemption for all taxpayers and a 50 per cent tax on all income over and above the exemption level. A person with a $1,000 income pays no tax; a person with a $2,000 income pays a 25% tax on his total income since he pays a 50% tax on the $1,000 over the exemption; similarly a man with $5000 pays an effective tax of 40%; and finally a man with $100,000 pays virtually a 50% tax on his total income.

This distinction between the progression arising from an exemption and other forms of progression is of more than technical interest. As a practical matter there appears to be no way of granting an exemption to the lowest income level in the community without producing the exemption type of progression in the effective rates for a large number of persons with incomes above the exemption level.[8] It is almost unanimously agreed that some exemption keyed to at least a minimum subsistence standard of living is desirable. Since such an exemption will necessarily result in some degree of progression among taxpayers above the exemption level, and since this degree of progression appears inescapable, the real issue is whether any added degree of progression can be justified. In our tax system it is usual to derive such added amount of progression through graduating the marginal rates of tax upwards; and in this framework the issue is whether graduated marginal rates can be justified.

With these qualifications the question of the essay can be finally formulated: On what grounds is a progressive tax on all incomes over a minimum subsistence exemption to be preferred to a proportionate tax on all incomes over a minimum subsistence exemption?[9]

[7] A popular error under our personal income tax is to confuse the marginal rate on the last increment of income and the effective rate on the total income and so to conclude, for example, that a taxpayer who reaches the 70% rate bracket is taxed at 70% on his total taxable income.

[8] See text, section 20 infra.

[9] In section 20 attention will be given to the possibility of obtaining the progression by raising the exemption substantially above a rigorously defined minimum subsistence level.

There might appear to be two shorthand ways of disposing of the question. It is not infrequently thought that under modern conditions progression in the personal income tax has become a revenue necessity. If the regular costs of operating government are now so large that it would not be possible to satisfy them through a merely proportionate tax on income, perhaps nothing further need be said. But this view appears to be based on an erroneous impression of how much of the revenue at the present time is produced exclusively by the graduation of rates. Something less than a quarter of the total revenue currently raised through the personal income tax is attributable to the graduated surtax rates, and there can be no doubt that it would be quite possible to obtain the same total through a personal income tax having a single basic rate.

A widely accepted argument for having some degree of progression in the federal income tax today is that it merely compensates for the regressivity of other taxes in our overall tax system.[10] Its function in this view is to make the total burden from *all* taxes proportionate to the incomes of taxpayers. There is a question whether in fact our federal income tax, which is steeply progressive, serves to do more than counterbalance the regressivity of the rest of the system. Two recent interpretations of the data have reached widely different conclusions on this score. One found that by and large our tax system is proportionate, with an element of progression appearing only at the top of the income scale.[11] The other found that over broad ranges of the income scale the tax system is highly progressive.[12] However, the discussion of the merits of progression does not depend on which is the better interpretation of the data. The significant

[10] Seligman has christened this the "special compensatory theory." Seligman, Progressive Taxation in Theory and Practice 146 (2d ed., 1909). There seems to be no dissent to this much progression, since of course it does not involve the adoption of the principle itself. See Lutz, Public Finance 363 (3d ed., 1936).

[11] "The over-all tax structure is by no means as progressive as is generally surmised, at least not as far as the lower 90 percent of the taxpayers are concerned. Rather, the effective rate curve follows a U-shaped pattern with regression at the lower end, a proportional range over the middle and progression at the upper end of the scale. Over a wide range of incomes, including 90 or more per cent of spending units, the progressive elements of the tax structure appear to be balanced or outweighed by others which are proportional or regressive." Musgrave, Carroll, Cook & Frane, Distribution of Tax Payments by Income Groups: A Case Study for 1948, 4 Nat'l Tax J. 1, 28 (1951).

[12] "[I]t appears to me to be established beyond doubt that the national system of taxation as a whole is highly progressive in the matter of rates from $1,000 up. This is especially true of federal taxation by itself. State and local taxes appear to be slightly progressive in the ranges of incomes between $1,000 and $15,000. Above $15,000 they are probably regressive in states that have no income taxes, or in which the highest income tax rate is less than 7 per cent, since the only state and local taxes that are clearly progressive above $10,000 in their effective rates are individual income taxes and inheritance taxes." Tucker, Distribution of Tax Burdens in 1948, 4 Nat'l Tax J. 283 (1951).

question is whether the tax system as a whole is intended to be proportionate or progressive, and the fact that controversy over progression usually focuses on the income tax should not be taken to mean that the question is being viewed that narrowly. There are relatively few taxes which can be vehicles for making the system as a whole progressive, and the income tax is probably the best of these.

3

Anyone who is aware of the extent to which philosophical, economic and jurisprudential questions are justiciable[13] under the American legal scheme would expect to find at least one great judicial consideration of the principle of progression. As late as 1916 the Yale Law Journal featured an article entitled, "The Constitutionality of the Graduated Income Tax Law," which began:

Whether under the constitutional power to levy a tax Congress may impose upon incomes of larger amounts a higher rate of tax than upon smaller incomes, is a question of very grave importance. The Tariff Act of 1913 . . . provides for levying . . . an additional income tax. This additional tax is commonly known as a 'surtax.' In the opinion of a great many lawyers this feature of the income tax law violates that principle of equality which requires that all taxable income, so far as amount is concerned, be treated alike.[14]

The article is perhaps most noteworthy because it appears to have been virtually the last gasp of constitutional objection to the principle of progression. By the time it was published the Supreme Court had disposed of all constitutional questions about progression and had done so with remarkably little discussion.

As is well known, the climax of the constitutional controversy in the United States over a federal income tax came in 1895 in the celebrated *Pollock* cases.[15] What is usually remembered about these cases is that the Supreme Court adopted the views of taxpayers' counsel that a tax on the income from real and personal property is a direct tax within the constitutional requirement that direct taxes be apportioned among the states, and that since these aspects of the tax were not separable the whole tax was unconstitutional.[16] But there was more to the cases than this.

[13] The phrase is taken from Pekelis, Law and Social Action (1950); see the review of this work in 19 Univ. Chi. L. Rev. 406 (1952).

[14] Hackett, 25 Yale L.J. 427 (1916).

[15] Pollock v. Farmers' Loan & Trust Co., 157 U.S. 429 (1895), rehearing 158 U.S. 601 (1895). An income tax with explicitly graduated rates, enacted during the Civil War, was held to be constitutional in Springer v. United States, 102 U.S. 586 (1880). The progressive feature of the tax, however, was not in controversy in that case.

[16] Undoubtedly the success of taxpayers' counsel in the Pollock cases marks a high point in American legal advocacy in view of the difficulties in arguing that an income tax was a direct

The tax in question, enacted in 1894, had a flat rate of 2% on income but allowed each individual taxpayer an exemption of $4,000. It was thus a tax which was substantially progressive in effective rates for all taxpayers who had incomes above the $4,000 exemption, and this progressivity was recognized in public discussions. In fact one of the most bitter attacks ever made against progression was directed against this tax.[17] In presenting their positions to the Court, counsel for the taxpayers, though placing their chief reliance on the direct tax point, did devote a substantial portion of their arguments to a second point. They argued that the tax, because of the various exemptions it contained, violated the constitutional requirement of uniformity of indirect taxes and contravened the due process clause of the Fifth Amendment.[18] A main target of this attack was the $4,000 exemption. On the issue of uniformity the Court divided four to four and therefore expressed no opinion. The dissenting opinions, of notable vigor and energy, likewise abstained from discussing the issue. Only in the concurring opinion of Justice Field is the question explored, and in his view the arbitrariness of the exemption would in itself have been a sufficient basis for invalidating the tax:

The income tax law under consideration is marked by discriminating features which affect the whole law. It discriminates between those who receive an income of $4000 and those who do not. It thus vitiates, in my judgment, by this arbitrary discrimination, the whole legislation. . . . The legislation, in the discrimination it makes, is class legislation. Whenever a distinction is made in the burdens the law imposes or in the benefits it confers on any citizens by reason of their birth, or wealth, or religion, it is class legislation, and leads inevitably to oppression and abuses, and to general unrest and to disturbance in society. . . . It is the same in essential character as that of the English income tax statute of 1691, which taxed Protestants at a certain rate, Catholics, as a class, at double the rate of Protestants, and Jews at another and separate rate.[19]

From the point of view of this essay, the arguments of taxpayers' counsel, although frequently vigorous in rhetoric, are of disappointingly little

---

tax. Seligman has subjected their scholarship to close and critical scrutiny in The Income Tax 531–89 (2d ed., 1921). The manner in which the unconstitutionality of the tax was argued perhaps is best reflected in a remark, during oral argument, by Attorney General Richard Olney: "It is a matter of congratulation, indeed, that the existence of the Constitution itself is not impeached, and that we are not threatened with a logical demonstration that we are still living, for all taxable purposes at least, under the regime of the old Articles of Confederation." Pollock v. Farmers' Loan & Trust Co., 157 U.S. 429, 513 (1895).

[17] Wells, The Communism of a Discriminating Income Tax, 130 North Amer. Rev. 236 (1880).

[18] See, for example, the argument of W. D. Guthrie, Pollock v. Farmers' Loan & Trust Co., 157 U.S. 429, 449 et seq. (1895).

[19] Ibid., at 596.

interest. Counsel tended to lump together the $4,000 exemption with the various exemptions granted by the law to charities and special corporations and to argue that it was an example of a family of arbitrary exemptions. Moreover, and perhaps more interesting for present purposes, counsel did not call attention to the fact that the tax was steeply progressive among the taxpayers having incomes over the exemption level. They noted only that the tax discriminated between the 98% of the population who would fall below the exemption level and the 2% who would pay the tax and that in this respect the tax was progressive as between the two groups. Quite probably it would have made no difference had taxpayers' counsel been more explicit about progression. Nevertheless, as the argument was framed the issue seemed to be merely that of the legislature's discretion to set the level of exemptions and not the more challengeable principle of progressive rates.[20]

At the federal level there are only three other relevant cases.[21] In 1898 the Illinois inheritance tax came before the Court in *Magoun v. Illinois Trust*.[22] The law provided for a graduated rate where property was inherited by remote relatives or strangers. This discrimination in rates was challenged under the equal protection clause of the Fourteenth Amendment. The Court, speaking through Justice McKenna, disposed of the contention in a summary fashion, holding that since inheritance had always been regarded as a special privilege created by the state, the state was free to condition its exercise as it saw fit. The Court added that the classification according to size of inheritance seemed reasonable, saying, "When the legacies differ in substantial extent, if the rate increases the benefit increases to a greater degree."[23] In a strong dissent Justice Brewer found that the abandonment of the proportionate principle rendered the tax clearly unequal and therefore unconstitutional. The vice, he said, was that it was "a tax unequal because not proportioned to the amount of the estate; unequal because based upon a classification purely arbitrary, to wit, that of wealth—a tax directly and intentionally made unequal."[24] In reaching this conclusion Justice Brewer stated that the majority seems to have "conceded that if this were a tax upon property such increase in the

---

[20] See the argument of James C. Carter, ibid., at 526.

[21] The constitutionality of progression under state constitutions has been raised with some frequency. The cases are reviewed in Crane, Progressive Income Taxes and Constitutional Uniformity of Taxation, 2 Pitt. L. Rev. 44 (1935). The cases are not helpful on the merits of the principle of progression.

[22] 170 U.S. 283 (1898).

[23] Ibid., at 300.   [24] Ibid., at 303.

rate of taxation could not be sustained";[25] and there are at least good grounds for doubting that the majority at that date would have sustained a progressive tax on property or income.

Two years later in *Knowlton v. Moore*[26] the Court upheld the federal inheritance tax of 1898. The tax contained graduated rates based on the amount of the inheritance. Justice White for the majority gave elaborate consideration to the contention that the graduated rates, among other features, violated the uniformity clause. His discussion, however, was pointed towards establishing that the clause required only geographical uniformity. It had been further contended in the argument that the progressive rates were "so repugnant to fundamental principles of equality and justice, that the law should be held to be void, even although it transgressed no express limitation in the Constitution."[27] Justice White dismissed this point simply by saying it was disposed of in the *Magoun* case. He then went on to add the most explicit comment ever made by the Court about progression:

The review which we have made exhibits the fact that taxes imposed with reference to the ability of the person upon whom the burden is placed to bear the same have been levied from the foundation of the government. So, also, some authoritative thinkers, and a number of economic writers, contend that a progressive tax is more just and equal than a proportional one. In the absence of constitutional limitation, the question whether it is or is not is legislative and not judicial. The grave consequences which it is asserted must arise in the future if the right to levy a progressive tax be recognized involves in its ultimate aspect the mere assertion that free and representative government is a failure, and that the grossest abuses of power are foreshadowed unless the courts usurp a purely legislative function. If a case should ever arise, where an arbitrary and confiscatory exaction is imposed bearing the guise of a progressive or any other form of tax, it will be time enough to consider whether the judicial power can afford a remedy by applying inherent and fundamental principles for the protection of the individual, even though there be no express authority in the Constitution to do so. That the law which we have construed affords no ground for the contention that the tax imposed is arbitrary and confiscatory, is obvious.[28]

It might be noted that Justice Brewer again dissented, remaining firm in his conviction that any progression was unconstitutional.

Even after the *Knowlton* case it was quite possible to argue that the question of the constitutionality of a progressive tax on income as contrasted to progressive death taxes had not been foreclosed. Nothing about progression had been decided in the *Pollock* case; the *Magoun* case turned on the complete discretion of a state to impose conditions on inheritance;

[25] Ibid., at 302.

[26] 178 U.S. 41 (1900).

[27] Ibid., at 109.

[28] Ibid., at 109–110.

and the *Knowlton* case, while containing general language that the issue of progression is a matter of economic controversy properly within the area of legislative discretion, primarily decided that progression did not violate the uniformity clause. And although the Court in the *Knowlton* case appeared to regard all other questions about the general equity of progression as having been disposed of by the *Magoun* case, there was in fact no discussion of such questions in the *Magoun* case.

With this background it is understandable that when the Court for the first time was confronted with progression in the form of an income tax with explicitly graduated rates, at least some of the bar thought that the question would compel extended discussion by the Court.[29] The issue was elaborately argued in 1915 in *Brushaber v. Union Pacific*,[30] dealing with the 1913 income tax, the first income tax enacted under the Sixteenth Amendment. But in his opinion Chief Justice White, speaking for a unanimous court, disposed of the question in a summary fashion. As in the *Knowlton* case it is apparent from the opinion that any argument about the constitutionality of progression was greatly handicapped because of the absence of a specific constitutional provision on which to bottom a broad challenge to its lack of equality. In the *Brushaber* case the Court first noted that the due process clause of the Fifth Amendment is not a limitation on the taxing power. But it then went on to observe:

It is true that it is elaborately insisted that although there be no express constitutional provision prohibiting it, the progressive feature of the tax causes it to transcend the conception of all taxation and to be a mere arbitrary abuse of power which must be treated as wanting in due process. . . . And over and above all this the contention but disregards the further fact that its absolute want of foundation in reason was plainly pointed out in *Knowlton v. Moore*, supra, and the right to urge it was necessarily foreclosed by the ruling in that case made. In this situation it is of course superfluous to say that arguments as to the expediency of levying such taxes or of the economic mistake or wrong involved in their imposition are beyond judicial cognizance.[31]

In the thirty-five years since the *Brushaber* case the issue of the constitutionality of progression has never been adverted to by the Court. There can be no doubt that progression today is immune from constitutional attack. It remains true however that the total wisdom the Court has

[29] Thus a notewriter in 1912 concluded that the death transfer tax cases were not conclusive in favor of the constitutionality of progression in an income tax. Progressive Income Taxes, 12 Col. L. Rev. 443 (1912). See also Hackett, The Constitutionality of the Graduated Income Tax Law, 25 Yale L.J. 427 (1916).

[30] 240 U.S. 1 (1916).

[31] Ibid., at 25. The opinion in the case is obviously colored by the Court's irritation with what it explicitly regarded as the many hypercritical contentions of taxpayers' counsel. Possibly the arguments as to progression would have fared better if they had been relied on alone.

offered on the merits of progression comes to the following: the one line observation of Justice McKenna in the *Magoun* case that (at least as to legacies) benefits increase to a greater degree than the rates; and the statements by Chief Justice White in the *Knowlton* and *Brushaber* cases that the issue is a matter of controversy in economics.

In retrospect the striking thing is not the result the Court reached, for the result seems clearly sound on constitutional grounds even when tested against current notions of substantive due process. Rather it is that the merits of progression as a principle were really never discussed by the Court.

4

The discussion of constitutional law has to some extent anticipated consideration of the political history of progression. Some further brief observations about that history are in order.

If one not informed about the history were simply to speculate as to what it had been, he would likely make the following conjectures: First, that as far as the taxation of income is concerned, the more controversial issue would have been the principle of progression and not the use of income as a tax base; second, that, unless the idea of progression had virtually always been a part of political thinking, it would be possible to locate and identify when and how it became widely accepted; third, that the political developments in England and the United States with respect to progression would have considerable influence on each other. While the definitive political history of progression has not as yet been written, the available information appears to indicate that none of these conjectures is well founded.

In both the United States and England progression was always in the shadow of the controversy of the income tax itself, and that controversy was bitter.[32] In the United States there was a brief experiment with an explicitly graduated tax on income during the Civil War.[33] The tax was generally regarded as an emergency war measure, and at the end of the war the graduated rates were repealed although the income tax itself remained in force until 1872. While after the war there was some separate

[32] The history is dealt with at length in Seligman, The Income Tax (2d ed., 1921); Ratner, American Taxation (1942). It is useful to note that the chief objections to adopting income as a base for measuring tax were that: (1) it would increase the possibility of fraud; (2) it would entail an undue invasion of the citizen's financial privacy; (3) it would be administratively cumbersome and costly; and (4) it would be unfair unless a differentiation in rates were made between income from different sources.

[33] Under the 1865 Act these rates reached 5 per cent on income in excess of $600 up to $5,000 and 10 percent on the excess over $5,000. The Confederacy enacted considerably steeper rates, the highest bracket being at 25 percent.

debate over progression, it is clear that it was subordinate to the central controversy over a tax on income. The next development was the 1894 Act, discussed in connection with the *Pollock* cases. It is worth noting that while that act restored a tax on income, explicit graduation was not again adopted and that there was progression only as a consequence of the $4,000 exemption. Nor do the debates indicate that there was any strong movement to introduce graduated rates into this tax. This sequence is further evidence that the Civil War experiment with graduation did not mean that the principle had won widespread public acceptance. The next great controversy was over the adoption of the Sixteenth Amendment itself and so was concerned chiefly with the propriety of income as a tax base. Again there was some subsidiary concern with progression and it was well recognized that it would be possible to have a graduated tax under the Amendment. But it was not until the first legislation under the Amendment, the Act of 1913, upheld in the *Brushaber* case, that the United States was committed to explicit graduation in taxing income. From 1913 to the present the progressive feature has been retained. Whatever the reasons, it seems that between 1894 and 1913 the deadline for sharp political debate over the progression principle had somehow passed.

The English development is strikingly parallel. An income tax was first introduced at the close of the eighteenth century as a temporary expedient to finance the war against Napoleon. The tax did not adopt explicit graduation of rates. While it did graduate exemptions according to the income of the taxpayer, it is quite clear that no one regarded this as other than a minor adjustment of the exemptions and not as an acceptance of the principle of progression.[34] This tax survived until 1816 and was constantly under fire. Once again the attack was almost wholly on the merits of income as a base. An income tax was not revived until 1842 and again it was understood to be a temporary tax. The debate over continuing it went on for a quarter of a century, being finally put to rest in 1874 with the defeat of Gladstone. During this period the adjustment for exemptions varied considerably in form and exact scope, but no one regarded them as a commitment to progression, and no government in office had favored progression.[35] By 1894 there had been a change. The Chancellor of the Exchequer then declared himself in favor of explicit

[34] Thus Pitt, who had introduced graduated abatements, was a staunch opponent of any further differentiation or graduation of rates. "It would be a presumptuous attempt to derange the order of society, which would terminate in producing confusion, havock, and destruction, and with a derangement of property, terminate in the overthrow of civilized life." 3 Speeches of the Rt. Hon. William Pitt in the House of Commons 14–15 (1808).

[35] "And, as is well known, the Income Tax was not charged on incomes of £150 per annum and less, whilst an abatement was allowed in respect of those above that sum but under

graduation but hesitated to recommend it for the income tax because of administrative difficulties.[36] For the next fifteen years the debate was primarily over the practical difficulties and there was growing acceptance of the principle on its merits.[37] When by 1909 the Lloyd George budget provided for graduated rates, it was once again apparent that the deadline for serious debate on the issue, this time in England, had passed. Since 1909 the principle has been retained in all subsequent income tax legislation.

Taxation seems to have been a rather provincial matter with each country working out its own system.[38] The instances of progression prior to the eighteenth century seem to have been too isolated and sporadic to have had influence on the English; and the French Revolution had only a deterrent effect on the proposing of progressive taxes, and even that

---

£400. But it cannot be said that these exceptions to the general rule were introduced from a deep-seated conviction of the justice or expediency of graduation; and it is probable that the authors of some of them would have expressly repudiated the principle, and have contended—if, indeed, they did not actually do so—that such principle was not involved in the schemes proposed. They were regarded rather as abnormal, if desirable, variations in the existing *régime*, than as introducing a different *régime;* and, although they formed quasi precedents and have helped to pave the way from the old order to the new, they aroused no great enthusiasm." Godard, Graduated Taxation, 5 Econ. Rev. 39 (1895).

[36] Seligman quotes the following from the budget speech of Sir William Vernon Harcourt of April 16, 1894: ". . . in principle there is nothing to be said against such a system [of graduated rates]; indeed, there is every argument in its favor. The difficulties which lie in its way are of an administrative and practical nature, which as yet I have not been able to find means to overcome." Seligman, The Income Tax 181 (2d ed., 1921).

[37] The Report from the Select Committee on Income Tax (1906) deals with the various administrative problems and concludes that further progression is "practicable" either through an extension of abatements or through the introduction of a super-tax on income above a certain amount. What troubled the Committee most about extending abatements was that the "total amount which was collected in excess of what was ultimately retained became so large as to cause serious inconvenience to trade and commerce and to individual taxpayers." The aspect of the super-tax which troubled the Committee most was whether the tax would work if based only on a personal declaration of income by the taxpayer. The English had used withholding at the source virtually since the beginning of their income tax, and the reluctance to compromise with the mechanism of collection at the source was a major obstacle to adoption of graduated rates. When the super-tax was finally adopted there was a compromise: collection at the source was retained for the basic tax but not extended to the super-tax. The present American system essentially makes the same compromise.

There had been at least mild concern with whether the taxpaying public could understand any formula by which graduated rates were set. This objection was cured by the use of the bracket system, and it amused Edgeworth, who observed: "Cannot the general public read the dial of a town clock without going behind to inspect the works?" II Edgeworth, Papers Relating to Political Economy 263 (1925). Two articles of interest in this connection are Burns, A Graduated Income Tax, 146 Westminster Rev. 555 (1896); Steggall, Note on Graduation of Income Tax, 25 Econ. J. 136 (1915).

[38] The history of progressive taxation is not confined to England and the United States. There are numerous instances going back at least to classical Greece; there is the radical experiment with progression during the French Revolution; there is the development of very elaborate schemes of progression on the Continent soon after the middle of the nineteenth century, particularly in some of the German states.

seems to have worn off quickly. When the United States adopted its Civil War act, it did not pattern it after the English model which had been available since 1842. Conversely, the English seemed to have paid little attention to this Civil War legislation. The 1894 experience in the United States likewise does not appear to have been affected much by the English developments up to that date. And the Continental experience was not an important political precedent in either England or the United States.

Progression has also had a considerable intellectual history and this will be examined in detail as part of the analysis of the principle on its merits. However, it is hard to trace a correlation between this intellectual development and the political history. It is a reasonably safe conjecture that the idea was not adopted at the popular level because it was widely thought that the intellectuals had perfected the case for it. During the last twenty years of the nineteenth century, which seems to be the decisive interval in public acceptance of the idea in England and the United States, the balance of theoretical discussion, insofar as it paid attention to the issue, was unfavorable to progression.[39] Certainly the most rigorous analysis of progression came only after the idea had become a political reality.

The reasons for this somewhat unexpected historical pattern are obscure. It may have been simply a consequence of the great widening of suffrage. It may have been a result of the increased concern with concentration of wealth, a concern confirmed by the passage of the Sherman Antitrust Act in 1890. It may have been produced by Socialist thinking in England and the Populist movement in the United States. It may have been due to the adoption of graduated death taxes as part of the move to limit inheritance. But whatever the reasons it is clear that the political history affords little insight into the merits of the principle of progression.

5

The affirmative case for progression has been rested on a variety of grounds. Before examining these it will be convenient to collect a group of considerations which can be offered as objections to progression regardless of the particular grounds urged in justification of it. These objections, while admittedly not conclusive in themselves, can be viewed as constituting a loose kind of prima facie case against the principle.

(a) The first such consideration is the price paid for progression in terms

---

[39] The lineup against progression prior to the turn of the century was impressive and included McCullough, J. S. Mill, Sidgwick, Bastable, Adams and Daniels.

of complicating the structure of the income tax, expanding the opportunity for taxpayer ingenuity directed to lawfully avoiding taxes, creating very difficult questions of equity among taxpayers, and obscuring the implications of any given provision in the tax law. It is remarkable how much of the day to day work of the lawyer in the income tax field derives from the simple fact that the tax is progressive. Perhaps the majority of his problems are either caused or aggravated by that fact. It may be useful and refreshing to reflect on what the positive law of income taxation would be like if the tax were a proportionate one. Any exemption in such a tax would, as has been pointed out, produce some progression; but the effects on positive law of an exemption set by a minimum subsistence standard would not be significant for present purposes and therefore can be ignored.

Under a flat tax no dollar tax difference turns on whether a certain income item or deduction item is properly to be charged to one person or to another. The advantage to taxpayers in splitting income among several taxable units in order to get it taxed in lower rate brackets is not present, since there is only one rate. The possibility of reducing taxes under progression by doing this has been the motivating factor for a large amount of taxpayer conduct. There is a long roster of familiar income-splitting devices which owe their existence to progression: the short term trust, the family partnership, the gift of bond coupons and dividends on shares, the assignment of anticipated earnings, much of the community property agitation, and many other stratagems.[40] It is thus progression which is the true father of such distinguished precedents in taxation as *Lucas v. Earl*,[41] *Corliss v. Bowers*,[42] *Burnet v. Wells*,[43] *Poe v. Seaborn*,[44] *Helvering v. Clifford*,[45] *Helvering v. Horst*,[46] and *Comm'r v. Culbertson*.[47]

With a flat tax it is a matter of indifference what the taxable unit is. But under a progressive system this issue poses an almost insuperably difficult problem of equity among taxpayers. The unit selected by the tax

[40] Definitive discussions of the family income splitting problem can be found in Surrey, Assignments of Income and Related Devices: Choice of the Taxable Person, 33 Col. L. Rev. 791 (1933); Miller, Gifts of Income and of Property: What the Horst Case Decides, 5 Tax L. Rev. 1 (1949); Bruton, Family Partnerships and the Income Tax—The Culbertson Chapter, 98 U. of Pa. L. Rev. 143 (1949); Alexandre, The Corporate Counterpart of the Family Partnership, 2 Tax L. Rev. 493 (1947); Surrey, Federal Taxation of the Family—the Revenue Act of 1948, 61 Harv. L. Rev. 1097 (1948); Treas. Dep't Study, The Tax Treatment of Family Income (1947).

[41] 281 U.S. 111 (1930).

[42] 281 U.S. 376 (1930).

[43] 289 U.S. 670 (1933).

[44] 282 U.S. 101 (1930).

[45] 309 U.S. 331 (1940).

[46] 311 U.S. 112 (1940).

[47] 337 U.S. 733 (1949).

system for comparing incomes will determine the size of income aggregates subject to tax, and the size of the income aggregates will determine the effective rates of tax. Different solutions to the unit problem will produce marked differences in the allocation of the tax burden. Yet there seem to be no criteria for deciding whether the unit ought to be the individual, the marital community, the family, the household or some other combination of persons. The controversy in the early forties over making it mandatory for married couples to combine their incomes in a single return;[48] the adoption in the late forties of an option for married couples to split their incomes evenly for tax purposes;[49] and the recent enactment of a provision giving some of the benefits of such a split to an unmarried person who is the head of a household,[50] all reflect the difficulty of finding a satisfactory formula.

Another cluster of issues considerably aggravated by progression concerns the proper timing of income and expense items. These issues can be characterized with approximate accuracy as those which an adequate system for the averaging of income would eliminate. Some of the factors that make timing significant taxwise are common to both proportion and progression. Changes in the rate of tax, or changes in the substantive tax law, or changes in the status of the taxpayer, or the operation of a statute of limitations would all make timing of significance taxwise. But the impact of these factors is likely to be much more serious under progression; and, these factors apart, progression always operates to make timing important. Under it income spread over several years results in a lesser aggregate amount of tax than the same amount of income bunched in one year. The splitting of income between different taxable years thus operates something like the splitting of income between different taxable persons. To an extent this accounts for the current popularity of discretionary family trusts and family corporations;[51] it also accounts for the great attention which is paid to accounting rules in allocating income between time periods.[52] And one of the few plausible arguments, if not the only one, for spe-

[48] See H.R. Rep. No. 1040, 77th Cong. 1st Sess. 10 et seq. (1941), accompanying the proposed Revenue Act of 1941.

[49] Int. Rev. Code § 12(d), 26 U.S.C.A. § 12(d) (1948) added by the Revenue Act of 1948.

[50] Int. Rev. Code § 12(c), 26 U.S.C.A. § 12(c) (Supp., 1951), added by the Revenue Act of 1951.

[51] See Arnold, Taxation of Income of Estates and Trusts, 6 Federal Bar Ass'n Series on Practical Aspects of Federal Taxation (1946); Johnson, Taxing Dividends of Family Corporations—A Dissent, 2 Tax L. Rev. 566 (1947).

[52] This was one of the points stressed by Simons. "[A]bsence of averaging rebates grossly overstrains the capacity of accounting (and of meticulous legalistic rules and fictions) for

cial treatment of capital gains stems from this characteristic of progression. Because a capital gain may have been in the making for many years, it seems unfair to tax all of it as the income of a single year.

This matter of the unit of time for tax purposes is like the problem of selecting the appropriate taxable unit, not only in strongly inviting taxpayer ingenuity but also in posing for the system new and serious questions of equity among taxpayers. One approach, currently adopted, is to make special provision for the hardest cases. The result has been a series of particularized "averaging" devices such as the net operating loss carry back and carry forward,[53] the spreading out of lump sum compensation,[54] the instalment sales method of reporting profit,[55] the last-in first-out inventory method,[56] and the carry over of capital losses.[57] Together these have enormously complicated the structure of the law. The other approach is to introduce a general averaging scheme so as to spread out all income evenly for tax purposes over a period of years. Although several schemes have been worked out in detail, and in some jurisdictions have actually been tried, none has won widespread support in connection with the federal income tax.[58] Each of the schemes necessarily involves technical complexity and increases administrative problems. More important, each of them raises new questions of equity among taxpayers. It is not obvious, for example, whether it is fairer to average the income of a person over his entire life, including his pre-earning and his retirement years, or

---

locating income precisely in time, i.e., for allocating income *between* short (annual) periods. All such allocations are inherently arbitrary or provisional. Because it makes them extremely important (definitive instead of provisional), current procedure under the law and Regulations is extremely faulty and weak." Simons, Federal Tax Reform 49–50 (1950).

See Introductory Note to c. 5, Surrey and Warren, Federal Income Taxation: Cases and Materials 287–92 (1950).

[53] Int. Rev. Code § 122, 26 U.S.C.A. § 122 (Supp., 1951).

[54] Int. Rev. Code § 107, 26 U.S.C.A. § 107 (Supp., 1951).

[55] Int. Rev. Code § 44, 26 U.S.C.A. § 44 (Supp., 1951).

[56] "If Lifo is not the most complicated of averaging schemes, and the least effective, my judgment on tax issues (as many readers will perhaps readily agree) is worthless. Any crude scheme of averaging rebates, not to mention flexibility in inventory procedure, would enable us to get rid of an unlovely contribution of uninspired statistical empiricists to our tax edifice." Simons, Federal Tax Reform 106 (1950). Cf. The Facts of Lifo, 44 Fortune 77 (Dec. 1951): "These bookkeeping policies have assumed such importance in relation to profits that what formerly was a bookkeeping matter is now a top-management problem."

[57] Int. Rev. Code § 117(e), 26 U.S.C.A. § 117(e) (1945).

[58] See Blough, Averaging Income for Tax Purposes, 20 Accounting Rev. 85 (1945); Vickrey Agenda for Progressive Taxation 164–95 (1947); Bravman, Equalization of Tax on All Individuals with the Same Aggregate Income Over a Number of Years, 50 Col. L. Rev. 1 (1950); Simons, Federal Tax Reform 40–44 (1950).

whether it is fairer to divide his life into certain arbitrary time intervals for averaging purposes.

Under a flat tax it is relatively easy to trace the immediate consequences on the distribution of the total tax burden of such things as credits based on a taxpayer's status, deductions for particular expenditures, and exclusions of particular kinds of income from the tax base. The impact on the taxpayer does not depend on the total amount of his income. With graduated rates the impact on any taxpayer depends in part on the rate bracket he is in. The exclusion of interest on state bonds furnishes a good example.[59] Under a flat tax this exclusion would serve only to permit the states to borrow at lower rates of interest than if the interest paid were taxable to the recipients. No purchasers of the bonds would benefit by the exclusion since, in a normal market, they would have to pay a premium equal to the value of the tax saved. The attractiveness of the bonds, relative to other securities, would not vary with the income of the investors. With progression the situation is different. The exempt bonds are relatively more attractive to persons with larger incomes, subject to higher rates of tax, than to persons with smaller incomes simply because the dollar tax savings to the former is greater. A state cannot sell all of its exempt bonds to persons in the highest tax bracket; the overall quantity of exempt bonds outstanding is so large that a new issue can be marketed only by interesting persons in lower brackets. This means that the premium to acquire such bonds will just equal the value of the tax savings to the lowest bracket purchaser. From this fact follow two important consequences which differ from those under a flat tax. The subsidy to the states will be larger than under a comparable flat tax, since the premium which the bonds can command will be larger because the aggregate tax savings to purchasers will be larger. And the purchasers above the middle bracket will get a substantial tax saving which no one would advocate for its own sake.

This instance has been examined in detail because it illustrates with special clarity how progression may complicate and obscure the operation of a seemingly simple provision. Progression tends to produce, as a by-product, consequences which probably are unintended and frequently are undesirable. Such obscurity is accentuated in a tax system which has been undergoing almost constant legislative change.

The price the tax system pays for progression is thus high. It produces a tax law of almost impenetrable complexity. It invites a distorting attention to the tax aspects of any economic transaction. It affords an excessive stimulus to tax avoidance with perhaps incalculable consequences for taxpayer morale and the general respect for law.

(b) A second basic objection to a progressive tax on income is that it is a politically irresponsible formula. Under any progressive system today the higher surtax rates are almost certain to apply only to a minority of voters. This means that a majority are allowed to set the rates which fall exclusively on the minority. No majority, so the argument runs, can pass fairly or responsibly on an issue so infected with its own immediate self interest. A proportionate tax on income presents no comparable weakness since each voter in voting taxes for others to pay necessarily votes an equivalent rate for himself.

In one form this objection, although forceful, simply restates the difficulties of majority rule in general. It is the very nature of majority rule that the majority can vote distinctive burdens for the minority, and it is clearly impossible to disqualify all "interested" voters. If nothing more can be found in this point against progression, it admits of a short and sufficient answer. Majority rule with all its difficulties is superior to any other principle for resolving group decisions. Not to agree with this preference for majority rule is to reject democratic self-government.[60]

---

[60] "Finally, a somewhat widespread objection to progressive taxation is contained in the argument which has been well put by Lecky (Democracy and Liberty, i, p. 287), when he tells us that highly graduated taxation realizes most completely the supreme danger of democracy, creating a state of things in which one class imposes on another burdens which it is not asked to share, and impels the state into vast schemes of extravagance under the belief that the whole cost will be thrown upon others. 'The belief is no doubt very fallacious, but it is very natural, and it lends itself most easily to the claptrap of dishonest politicians. Such men will have no difficulty in drawing impressive contrasts between the luxury of the rich and the necessities of the poor, and in persuading ignorant men that there can be no harm in throwing great burdens of exceptional taxation on a few men, who will still remain immeasurably richer than themselves.' "

"The same point has been urged by an American, Mr. W. D. Guthrie, in an argument opposing the constitutionality of the so-called 'Dudley Bill' passed by the Legislature of New York in 1897, providing for a progressive inheritance tax, and which was in consequence vetoed by Governor Black. (Argument of William D. Guthrie, submitted to the Hon. Frank S. Black, Governor of the State of New York, in opposition to the Dudley Bill, 1897, pp. 16, 17). 'The great danger of all democracies,' says Mr. Guthrie, 'is that one class votes the taxes for another class to pay. Heretofore, our bulwark has been that, as all taxes were equally and uniformly imposed, classes could not be discriminated against, and this protected all. . . . Introduce the policy of graduated taxes, establish the doctrine that they are permissible under our system, and the whole burden of taxation can be thrown on a few rich.' To this argument, which is obviously political rather than economic in character, it may be replied that the fears here expressed have not been realized in practice, and that the reasoning, if carried to its logical conclusion, would result in a complete distrust of democratic government as such. There is no advantage in conjuring up fanciful dangers which have been disproved by ex-

But the objection may cut more deeply if it can be shown that the possibility of majority exploitation of a minority is so great in allocating tax burdens as to require limiting the jurisdiction of the majority. It is another characteristic of democracy, coordinate in importance with majority rule, that there are some decisions which cannot be entrusted to any majority.[61] In our society these have been given explicit constitutional status, as for example freedom of speech and religion. There is, as already noted, no explicit constitutional prohibition against progressive taxation, and there has been no tendency to develop one implicitly on broad constitutional grounds, such as due process. But the objection to unfettered majority rule in taxation may be a way of saying that if there is not a constitutional limitation on the majority's power, there ought to be one because of the special weakness of the minority's position. It may be thought that tax legislation is class legislation in its most naked form. Unlike most instances of legislation by majority rule, it might appear here that there cannot be an element of bargaining or compromise; the majority may think it can lose nothing in lightening its own tax burden at the expense of the wealthier minority. Such legislation becomes tantamount, so the argument goes, to a taking of property without compensation.

To the objection thus elaborated there are several answers. Whatever the reasons, the history does not bear out the prediction of unbridled use of the majority's power to tax.[62] Furthermore, in a fluid society like ours membership in the majority and minority is not a permanent matter. Everyone hopes to get into the surtax brackets tomorrow and not a few succeed. In any event there seems to be widespread recognition of the fact that at some level highly progressive taxes will impair important economic incentives and thereby affect the whole community adversely.

It is easy to overstate this political objection to progression. Essen-

---

perience." Seligman, Progressive Taxation in Theory and Practice 297–98 (2d ed., 1909). See also Bastable, Public Finance 306 (3d ed., 1922).

Cf. the observation of Chief Justice White, previously quoted in the text, in section 3 supra, from Knowlton v. Moore. "The grave consequences which it is asserted must arise in the future if the right to levy a progressive tax is recognized involves in its ultimate aspect the mere assertion that free and representative government is a failure. . . ." 178 U.S. 41, 109 (1900).

[61] The ultimate statement of this point is Mill's famous remark. "If all mankind minus one were of one opinion, and only one person were of the contrary opinion, mankind would be no more justified in silencing that one person, than he, if he had the power, would be justified in silencing mankind." Mill, On Liberty 79 (Everyman ed., 1925).

[62] It is worth noting that there have been occasions on which rates have become less progressive. This occurred during the Coolidge administration and again under the so-called Knutson tax reduction plan after World War II.

tially the point is that, just as progression poses difficult problems of equity among taxpayers which need not otherwise arise, so it places strains on the majority rule principle which perhaps need not otherwise arise.

(c) A third line of objection to progression, and undoubtedly the one which has received the most attention, is that it lessens the economic productivity of the society. Virtually everyone who has advocated progression in an income tax has recognized this as a counterbalancing consideration; in fact the most perceptive discussions of the point have been offered by persons who were friendly to progression.[63] The degree to which progression tends to lower productivity is inherently difficult to gauge. For the most part it would appear to depend upon the effect which progression has on the motivations of men, and most of what can be said on either side is in the realm of conjecture in psychology and is likely to remain there.[64]

Unless the problem is carefully stated, it is easy to saddle the special case for progression with the undesirable economic consequences which flow from high taxes generally. It is worth a reminder that the disadvantages of progression, as well as its advantages, in this connection and in all others, are to be assessed only by contrasting a progressive system which raises a given amount of revenue to a proportionate one which raises an identical amount of revenue. The distinctive impact of progression on productivity, as distinguished from high taxes generally, lies in two factors. The first is that a minority of the population will be subjected to higher effective rates of tax than would otherwise obtain. This minority is likely to be of special importance economically. The second relates to the accelerating marginal rates under a tax with graduated rates. In dealing with economic motivations one almost necessarily must be employing some sort of incremental analysis. The persons who are making the decisions are themselves likely to be thinking in terms of marginal units of reward and marginal units of effort. Graduated tax rates tend to result in a superimposition of increasing tax rates upon the natural curve of decreasing willingness to work more.

Progression basically may impinge on the productivity of the society either by reducing the amount or quality of work put forth or by impeding the creation or maintenance of capital in the society. The analysis

[63] See particularly Carver, The Ethical Basis of Distribution and Its Application to Taxation, 6 Annals 95 et seq. (July 1895); III Edgeworth, Papers Relating to Political Economy, 104 et seq. (1925); Pigou, A Study in Public Finance, c. V–VI (3d ed., 1951); Simons, Personal Income Taxation 19 et seq. (1938).

[64] There have, however, been some significant empirical studies; see Kimmel, Taxes and Economic Incentives, c. 4 (1950).

therefore must be concerned with motivations to work and with the various motivations responsible for the creation and preservation of capital.

Perhaps the most conspicuous group whose efforts are likely to be affected by high marginal tax rates are the possessors of talents which are highly rewarded by the market. It is not difficult to concede that money is the dominant stimulus to work in our society. The desire for money, however, obviously competes with other factors such as the preference for leisure, the nonmonetary attractiveness and unattractiveness of particular kinds of work to a given individual, and the personal "costs" of working, including fatigue and anxiety. It follows that when the monetary reward is reduced by taxation the other factors necessarily carry relatively greater weight in determining a person's actions. In the aggregate the tendency of progression is to cause talented persons to prefer leisure more and to shift to work which in its nonmonetary aspects they regard as more attractive but which society, as measured by its monetary rewards, has regarded as less important.

The difficulty, however, is that there is no way of measuring how strong this tendency is, and in any event there are some minimizing considerations. By and large the most attractive jobs are also the best paid. It is surely true that "what competing firms must pay to get experts away from one another is vastly different from what society would be obliged to pay in order to keep the experts from being ditch diggers."[65] Moreover, at some point it is doubtful if the attractiveness of additional income continues to be primarily a matter of having money. Rather money seems to become important as a symbol of prestige or success. Progression does not impair this incentive since the highest income is still the highest income both before and after taxes however high the marginal rate of tax.[66] And

[65] Simons, Personal Income Taxation 20 (1938).

[66] "Our captains of industry (enterprisers) are mainly engaged not in making a living but in playing a great game; and it *need* make little difference whether the evidence of having played well be diamonds and sables on one's wife or a prominent place in the list of contributors under the income tax. Besides—and this may be emphasized—the mere privilege of exercising power is no mean prize for the successful enterpriser." Ibid.

John Dewey has made the point with equal gusto, albeit for a somewhat different purpose. "Industrial leaders combine interest in making far-reaching plans, large syntheses of conditions based upon study, mastery of refined and complex technical skill, control over natural forces and events, with love of adventure, excitement and mastery of fellow-men." Dewey, Human Nature and Conduct 146 (Modern Library ed., 1930).

Observations such as these perhaps raise the larger issue of whether nonmonetary rewards might be substituted in whole or part for the present system. This matter has of course long been part of the debate over socialism. It would at least seem likely that the chances of establishing social esteem and prestige as the primary stimuli to work would be different under a regime that had abolished private property and enterprise.

there is some plausibility to the notion that being subject to higher tax rates may even be an inducement to persons to work harder in order to maintain their net position after taxes.

The largest part of the working force does not require consideration here since they are not likely to be subject to substantial graduation.[67] However, there may well be a group of the more skilled workers who would be in such surtax brackets, as appears to be the case at the present time. It is this group which would probably be most vulnerable to the deterrent effects of progression inasmuch as their nonmonetary rewards are not likely to be as great as those going to the more handsomely rewarded talents. But this group will be at the bottom of the graduated scale where the progression is least severe.

The impact of progression on the creation of capital is more complex. For present purposes the process of forming real capital in our society can be divided analytically into two distinct decisions upon which progression might have somewhat different bearing.[68] The first is the decision to invest in new or expanding enterprises to enable them to purchase capital goods, such as plants or machinery or inventory. The second is the decision to save rather than to consume, that is, to spend less than the total amount of one's income.

What is special about the decision to invest is that it is a decision to take risks. A major aspect of the impact of progression on productivity is to be found in its effects on risk taking. Progression changes the odds on the risk involved in all investments, and the change is always in the direction of making them less attractive. While the limitations which our present income tax system has imposed on the deduction of losses ag-

[67] The following observations of Pigou are of interest here:

"With the great majority of people, once their occupation is decided upon, the quantity of work which they do is only to a very limited extent within their own control. Their hours are fixed by rule; the intensity of their efforts in many cases by custom and tradition; their age of retirement by pension arrangements. It is only a comparatively small number of persons for whom the question often arises: 'Is it worth my while to do this extra piece of work, in view of the fact that, if I do, a part of the proceeds will be taken away in taxation?' The Minority of the Committee on National Debt and Taxation write: 'In the large and growing field of salaried enterprise (as contrasted with the medical, legal and such other professions as are usually remunerated by fees) both work and remuneration (and frequently also the age of retirement) are fixed, and the taxpayer cannot earn more by working harder or longer so to compensate for his increased taxation; nor can he reduce his liability to pay taxes by diminishing his output of work, unless he gives up his employment altogether. With the growth of joint-stock enterprise it appears to us that the case of the taxpayer who can and does adjust his output of work in accordance with his liability for taxation is so exceptional that it cannot now have any serious effect upon the total national output of productive work!'" Pigou, A Study in Public Finance 69–70 (3d rev. ed., 1951).

[68] Kimmel, Taxes and Economic Incentives 72–73 (1950).

gravates the bias against risk taking,[69] a simple illustration will demonstrate that the bias is inherent in the progression itself. Assume that a potential investor at present in the 40% tax bracket on the basis of his existing income foresees the opportunity of making $100,000 before taxes by investing $100,000 and calculates that the chances of success are even. Assume further that if the venture is successful the $100,000 profit would be taxed at an average rate of 70%; and that if the $100,000 invested in the venture were lost the loss could be deducted against the investor's other income which is being taxed at rates of 40% and lower. After taxes the investor stands to gain only $30,000 and to lose a net of over $60,000. Manifestly the odds on the investment have radically deteriorated after taxes.[70]

The extent to which this deterioration is due to the action of the progressive feature can be seen by considering a parallel case under a flat tax of 50% which will, it is assumed, raise the same amount of revenue in the aggregate. Under· such a tax the calculus after taxes is a $50,000 gain against a $50,000 loss. The ratio of estimated gain to estimated loss is thus not affected by the tax. To be sure, the high rate of tax itself might well discourage the making of the investment. But the impact of this factor, too, is magnified under a progressive system. It is the relatively wealthy who are an important source of investment funds in our society, and under progression they are taxed at rates higher than the single rate which would prevail under a comparable proportionate tax.

All investment entails some element of risk and therefore progression tends to hold down the magnitude of investment in the society. But the degree of risk attached to investments varies widely. Insofar as progression changes the odds against winning, the force of its tendency to discourage investment varies directly with the riskiness of the investment. By the same token it tends to create a preference for investing funds in

[69] There are three principal ways in which the present system discriminates against losses: capital losses cannot be deducted in full, a limitation which is particularly important for investments in unsuccessful corporate enterprises; operating losses can be carried backward and forward for only a limited number of years; there is no general averaging scheme and therefore the losses may come in the "wrong" year. See Simons, Federal Tax Reform 16–28 (1950).

[70] This is not to overlook the fact that under the current high rates of progression many expenditures are made in business which would not otherwise be made. Such expenditures may be instances of quasi-personal consumption by the businessman which are channelled through the business so as to be paid for with "cheap tax dollars." Or they may be instances of expenditures for good will or long range research which are made now in the expectation that the profits will be realized at a time when tax rates are lower or in the expectation that the profits will escape full taxation via the capital gains route. The first of these factors would appear also to operate under a proportionate tax, however.

debt securities rather than in equities. Progression thus tends to make it more difficult to obtain venture capital funds[71] and therefore to accentuate economic instability insofar as debt obligations are rigid and do not respond readily to general economic adjustments.[72]

It is one thing to trace out the repressive implications of progression on investment. It is quite another to assess their force because unquestionably there are many other influences at work in shaping the decisions of potential investors. Concern with inflation and deflation, the international situation, domestic political issues, changing patterns in institutional investing, and finally sheer habit all play a part.[73] And it may well be that a sufficient group in the society will be disposed to gamble whatever the odds. In any event it cannot be taken for granted that the discouragement of the most risky enterprises is, at our present level of technological development, an unqualified evil.

Ultimately the creation of capital is dependent on the willingness of people to save rather than consume. Progression may have an effect upon the decision to save in that it progressively lowers the effective rate of return on savings, that is, the rate after taxes. The impact of progression here is obviously analogous to the impact of progression on the incentive to work. There is a difference, however. In the case of the incentive to work the decreasing monetary rewards for working compete with nonmonetary factors such as leisure, the personal "cost" of work, and so forth. In the case of the incentive to save, the monetary reward for saving and thereby having money in the future competes with enjoying the use of the money now. However uncertain is our knowledge about the effects of progression on the incentive to work, it is even less certain as to the incentive to save. By reducing the effective rate of return on savings, progression might cause individuals to prefer to consume now. On the other hand it

[71] It has been suggested that it might be possible to retain progressive rates in general but tailor the tax structure so as to deliberately discriminate in favor of venture capital. Musgrave, Federal Tax Reform in Public Finance and Full Employment, Federal Reserve System, Postwar Economic Studies No. 3, 29–30 (1945). Even if one could be sure that the subsidy would go to the right places, such proposals raise serious problems of fairness among taxpayers.

[72] See for example Jones, Investment Prospects, 2 J. of Finance 15 (1947); Fisher, Booms and Depressions (1932).

[73] Today a substantial part of investment is financed out of retained corporate earnings. It is true that under the present tax structure such earnings are not subject to the progressive rates of the personal income tax, and this in part accounts for the magnitude of undistributed corporate profits. But such immunization is not an inherent feature of an income tax in a society with corporations.

The increasing importance of insurance companies as investors and of the investment trust may well lead to changing investment habits.

seems equally plausible that the lower effective rates will induce some persons to consume less now and to save and invest more in order to maintain their incomes after taxes at desired levels in the future.

The effects of progression on the incentive to work, on the incentive to take risks and on the incentive not to consume thus all appear to be highly indeterminate. In each case progression probably tends to reduce the incentive somewhat, but in each case the complexity of total motivation is such that substantial offsetting influences are present. There is, however, one final consequence of progression bearing on the formation of capital which is incontrovertible and substantial. It turns on the inescapable fact that the larger the income people have the more likely it is that they will save some part of it.[74] The steeper the progression the more probable it is that the tax money will come out of what would have been saved rather than out of what would have been consumed. This again is ultimately a matter of motivation, and to some extent the rich reduce their consumption rather than their savings under the pressure of higher taxes; but there can be no doubt that the net effect of a progressive tax as contrasted to a comparable proportionate tax is to reduce the total of savings. The progressive tax relieves the less wealthy of a certain amount of tax and transfers the burden of that amount to the more wealthy. The only relevant comparison for present purposes is the degree to which each of the two groups would spend or save out of *that* amount. It cannot be denied that a shift of the tax burden to the wealthy does result in a significant diminution of savings, and therefore the potential for capital creation, in the society as a whole.[75]

[74] "Nevertheless, it is hardly questionable that increasing progression is inimical to saving and accumulation. Under an individualistic system, great inequality is necessary to rapidly increasing indirectness in the productive process—necessary to the increasing use of resources in the production of more (and different) resources. The cost of our present stock of productive instruments was, in a significant sense, decades and centuries of terrible poverty for the masses. Conversely, the cost of justice will be a slowing-up in our material advance (though this effect may be modified if and as governments assume the role of savers).

"Increasing progression means augmenting incomes where saving is impossible and diminishing incomes too large to be used entirely for consumption. Thus, it means diversion of resources from capital-creation to consumption uses. The classes subject to the highest rates will not greatly curtail consumption; and persons at the bottom of the income scale, paying smaller taxes, will use their additional income largely to improve their standard of life. Some curtailment of consumption at the upper end of the scale may be expected, as may some increase of saving at the lower end. That the net effect will be increased consumption, however, hardly admits of doubt." Simons, Personal Income Taxation 22–23 (1938).

[75] Under a socialist regime this point has less force since the government can make direct provision for the accumulation of capital. It has also been suggested that such capital creation by government is not incompatible with a private enterprise economy. See Simons, Personal Income Taxation 26–30 (1938). The difficulty however is that it automatically and permanently enlarges the role of government.

As good as this point is, it frequently has been overstated as an objection to progression. There is sometimes a failure to note whether the concern is over preserving our existing accumulation of capital or maintaining or accelerating the rate at which capital has been formed in the past.[76] Everything indicates that it would take an extremely drastic rate of progression and very high taxes to endanger the existing accumulation of capital. If the concern is with the rate of growth of capital in the future the issue looks different: at some point it is reasonable to question the wisdom of society in always continuing to postpone present consumption for the sake of greater consumption tomorrow.

Furthermore, although greater productivity is undoubtedly a good and therefore greater savings is a good, it by no means follows that capital accumulation is always the overriding consideration.[77] A regressive tax system would be even more efficacious in promoting savings, but surely in our society the proposal to have such a system would give way before considerations of justice among taxpayers.[78] This is sufficient evidence

[76] "Since the revenues collected through progressive taxation are not applied to capital creation, but are spent for current operations or for non-reproductive durable goods, the effect is, inevitably, a depletion of the nation's capital fund. It would be in some degree justifiable to eat our seedcorn of capital if we were in such desperate straits that survival depended on this course. We are not in this plight. We are strong and wealthy. To eat the seedcorn under the illusion that we are thereby permanently bettering the condition of the people is a ghastly fiscal tragedy." Lutz, Some Errors and Fallacies of Taxation as Exemplified by the Federal Income Tax, National Tax Association, Proceedings of the 34th Annual Conference 371–73 (1941).

Lutz has suggested that progression would have prevented or retarded the mass production of Ford automobiles. "The American people face a serious choice here. . . . Concretely and in terms of an historical parallel, it is the choice between the Ford fortune and the Ford automobile. If they should decide that there shall be no more fortunes, they will also thereby decide that there shall be no more commodities of mass comfort and enjoyment other than those now known." Lutz, Guideposts to a Free Economy 82 (1945). This insight about Fords also came to Lord Hundson. See Hundson, Graduated Taxation and Industry, 39 The English Rev. 504, 507 (1924).

[77] It has not infrequently been argued that progression has some tendencies to increase productivity which will offset to some degree its negative impact on productivity. All of these plus factors flow from the greater equality of distribution under progression and might be treated as further arguments for equality on welfare grounds. See text, section 16 infra. Thus it is urged that there would be a tendency toward increased productivity: (1) because of the greater efficiency of the less wealthy resulting from an increase in their expenditures on health and education; (2) because of the improved morale resulting from the distribution and from its impact on industrial democracy; (3) because of the increased mobility of labor which may result from better education; (4) because of an increase in the savings of the less wealthy. It is probable that the first three of these consequences require, in addition to progression on the tax side, welfare expenditures for health and education. II Edgeworth, Papers Relating to Political Economy 105 (1925); Pigou, Economics of Welfare, Part V, c. 7, 9 (1920); Wedgwood, The Economics of Inheritance 25–34 (1929).

[78] A progressive spendings tax has been suggested as a way of retaining progression without impairing the incentive to save. Beale, The Measure of Income for Taxation, 19 J. of Pol. Econ. 655 (1911). Such a tax would inevitably be somewhat regressive at the higher levels of the income scale.

that the drawbacks of progression in terms of productivity must be weighed against its possible merits in allocating the tax burden fairly. It is not an adequate answer that those whose tax burden is greater under proportion than under progression will eventually benefit from the increased productivity of the society. The question remains, will they benefit enough?[79]

6

The objections to progression on the grounds that it greatly complicates the positive law of taxation, that it is conducive to political irresponsibility, and that it dampens incentives, while not without force, are far from conclusive:[80] If a strong case for progression can be made out affirmatively, these objections would not stand in the way. But if the doubts about the affirmative case for progression increase, these objections would take on greater weight.

The affirmative case has been rested on a variety of grounds, not all of which are compatible. Students who have reached a conviction in favor of progression have invariably done so on the basis of one analysis or another and not because of the cumulative impact of the various lines.[81] Most of the arguments for progressive taxation of income have been in terms of the

[79] "It is important to recognize that each generation inherits a system of property rights, as well as a stock of means of production—that it receives its resources with mortgages attached. If we deliberately limit the degree of progression, out of regard for effects on accumulation, we are in effect removing taxes from those who consume too much and transferring them to classes which admittedly consume too little; and against the additional capital resources thus painfully acquired are mortgages, property rights, in the hands of those freed from tax. While the saving will really have been done by those at the bottom of the income scale, those free from tax and their assigns will enjoy the reward. This method of fostering increase in productive capacity thus increases the concentration of property and aggravates inequality.

"If the productivity of capital were highly elastic—if the long-period demand for investment funds were not extremely elastic—the phenomenon of diminishing returns might be relied upon to mitigate the distributional effects. The masses would surely participate to some extent in the blessings of greater productive capacity. In fact, however, the scheme looks a bit like taxing small incomes to reduce consumption in the hope that those relieved of tax will save more after consuming all they can, and then allowing 1 per cent to those who have really done the saving and 4 per cent to those who have served merely by paying smaller taxes." Simons, Personal Income Taxation 25–26 (1938).

[80] At one time a fourth standard objection to progression was that it would be difficult to administer, especially in view of the added stimulus to tax evasion. See for example Bastable, Public Finance 310 (3d ed., 1922). No doubt high surtax rates are a stimulus to evasion, a point re-enforced perhaps by recent disclosures about the Bureau of Internal Revenue. But under modern administrative techniques this is not a problem of serious magnitude. And it is a somewhat embarrassing objection for those who bear the heaviest burden of the surtax to advance. It is true however, as noted in the prior section of the text, that progression has contributed mightily to the proliferation of tax avoidance schemes, with the consequence of greatly complicating the tax law.

[81] An exception perhaps is Sir Josiah Stamp in his Fundamental Principles of Taxation (1921).

justice with which it distributes the total tax burden. Such justifications in terms of distributional effects, although widely varying in theory, have one thing in common. They assume that by and large a tax on income is a burden on the taxpayers who are charged with the income and that it is not shifted by them to others. In other words it is assumed that the real incidence of the income tax is essentially the same as the burdens prescribed by the tax law. Analysis of the incidence of taxes has proved a very formidable problem as to which there has been a wide difference of expert opinion. In the main however it has been agreed that personal income taxes are probably not shifted to any substantial degree, at least not to a degree sufficient to disturb the positive arguments for progression.[82] Accordingly in this essay it is assumed that the burden of a tax on the incomes of persons is not shifted. And in any case, whether or not the shifting of the real burden of the tax is significant, the question of principle as to how the real burden should be allocated remains.

7

It may be appropriate to ignore the historical sequence in which ideas about progression were developed and to look first to the latest theories which, although they came too late to influence the initial acceptance of progression, probably have attracted the greatest amount of interest in more recent years.[83] It was not until the depression of the thirties that these theories were fully elaborated. The theories in brief seek to support a progressive tax on income in terms of the contribution such a tax can make to maintaining a high and stable level of economic activity.[84]

One approach[85] has proceeded by making a virtue out of what at one time was widely regarded as a principal weakness of any income tax, namely that it is likely to result in wide fluctuations of annual revenues.

[82] See the summary by Gillim of conflicting views regarding the incidence of a general income tax in The Incidence of Excess Profits Taxation 11–34 (1945), reprinted in Groves, Viewpoints on Public Finance 115–29 (1947).

To the extent that one accepts the negative impact of progression on economic incentives, outlined in section 5 of the text, one recognizes indeterminate secondary consequences of the tax which may affect the real burden of the tax.

[83] Adams, writing in 1898, in his discussion of progression refers to the impact of progression on purchasing power as a possible defense for progression. Adams, The Science of Finance 350–51 (1898).

[84] A brief survey of the various theories is contained in Blum, Tax Policy in a Democratic Society, 2 Nat'l Tax J. 97 (1949).

[85] This approach has been developed in the following literature: Mints, Monetary Policy, in Symposium on Fiscal and Monetary Policy, 28 Rev. of Econ. Statistics 60 (1946); Friedman, A Monetary and Fiscal Framework for Economic Stability, 38 Amer. Econ. Rev. 245 (1938); Simons, Rules versus Authorities in Monetary Policy, in Economic Policy for a Free Society 160 (1948); Mints, Monetary Policy for a Competitive Society (1950).

Collections under an income tax obviously will closely vary with changes in the level of economic activity. It is easy to show that the fluctuations in revenue from year to year under an income tax will be more marked than under a tax of comparable magnitude levied on property or on major items of consumption or even on consumer spending generally.[86] The instability of collections under an income tax will be increased even further if the rates are made progressive. Progression has the effect of changing the average effective rate of tax as incomes in general move up or down. As economic activity and therefore incomes decline, the average effective rate of tax will decline because of the movement of at least some taxpayers from the higher to the lower brackets. Conversely, in periods of rising economic activity the average effective rate will increase. The steeper the degree of progression the more sensitive will be these responses of the tax.

So long as a prime objective of fiscal policy was thought to be the balancing of the government budget each year, instability of the annual revenues could only be viewed as a disadvantage. To avoid having government deficits or surpluses it would be necessary to change frequently the level of government expenditures or the rates of tax. There is now however general agreement that it is altogether appropriate for the government deliberately to operate with an unbalanced budget whenever significant inflation or deflation is taking place. Operating with a deficit in times of deflation will inject spending power into the economy and tend to stem the deflation; operating with a surplus in times of inflation will withdraw spending power from the economy and tend to stem the inflation. The effect of an income tax, and particularly a progressive income tax, is always to change the level of revenue collections in the right direction. If government expenditures are kept constant, the tax will automatically produce a deficit or a surplus at the time one is needed. And if government expenditures are varied with a view to compensating for changes in the general level of economic activity, the income tax will always be a desirable complement.

The compensatory operations of the income tax would seem to be a desirable feature whatever the strategy for handling short run changes in economic activity. But the automaticity of such operations has had special appeal to those economists who have been interested in keeping to a minimum the range and significance of discretionary action by government authorities, particularly in times of distress. In their view the distinctive

---

[86] Even as to a general spendings tax the point holds because as the level of economic activity and therefore the level of income declines, aggregate expenditures do not decline at the same rate.

thing about a progressive income tax in this respect is that it changes the average effective rate of tax as needed, without requiring any official to institute that change and without waiting for him to do so. For those who have confidence in the ability of monetary policy to cope adequately with economic disturbances, the arrangement has additional advantages. It does not require government spending for the sake of spending during deflation, and it minimizes the possibility of discretionary action over-compensating for the change which has occurred.

It is easy to understand why this line of analysis has not been offered as an independent defense for progression. There is no reason for believing that the magnitude of the contribution of progression to economic stability is substantial. There are obvious limits on how much the progressive feature can add to the sensitivity of an income tax to economic changes. Furthermore the cost of dropping the progressive feature would be at most a modest increase in the use made of discretionary authority to change tax rates. Thus while progression may be of some help in maintaining economic stability, its advantages as a self-adjusting device are neither substantial nor indispensable.

Another and considerably different line of analysis appears at first to offer a more vigorous support for the progressive income tax as an antidote to depression. For this approach the important fact is not that progression makes the revenue collections more sensitive to economic changes, but rather that by definition a progressive income tax takes relatively more from the higher incomes and relatively less from the lower incomes than does any alternative pattern of tax. In this way the tax leaves the wealthy with relatively less income and the not-so-wealthy with relatively more. The implications of this fact for the level or stability of economic activity have been explored in several closely related contexts.

There is first what was once conceived to be the problem of economic stagnation in a mature economy.[87] In the late twenties the theory was offered that in a mature capitalist society an economic equilibrium could be reached only at a level at which there was substantially less than full employment of resources. At the heart of this theory was the hypothesis that in such a society opportunities for investment would have permanently declined to an extent that the amount spent on investment plus the amount spent on consumption would not support a high level of economic activity.[88] One obvious prescription was to raise the propensity of the so-

[87] This theory was given prominence by Lord Keynes in his General Theory of Employment, Interest, and Money (1936).

[88] "The essential points explaining the supposed chronic tendency of industry to run at low speed may be summarized as follows: First, in a wealthy community with shrinking oppor-

ciety to consume. As noted in the discussion of incentives and capital accumulation, the proportion of savings to total income of individuals increases on the average as their income increases. To raise the propensity of the society to consume, it was proposed to take income from the higher income classes which saved relatively more and transfer it to the lower income classes which saved relatively less. And this is what a progressive income tax in effect would do.

Accepting for the moment that stagnation is a problem, there are for our purposes two points to note about the proposed solution. First, in calling for shifting of income to raise the propensity to consume, it relies on the assumption that such shifting will not disturb the existing ratios of savings to total income of individuals at each income level. This is plausible, but it must remain something of a conjecture. It is not improbable that a large scale shifting of populations to different income levels would have some effect on the consumption and savings habits that theretofore obtained at those levels. Second, the anticipated increase on the consumption side will raise the level of economic activity in the society only if it does not entail an offsetting decrease on the investment side. While an anticipated increase in the level of consumer spending may improve the outlook for investment, there is the counterbalancing tendency of the progressive rates to deter risk taking and therefore investment.[89] However, the decisive thing about this solution to the problem of stagnation, as a defense for progression, is that it solves a problem which no longer is so widely thought to exist. Events in the past decade seem to show there is no permanent dearth of opportunities for investment.

tunities for new investment, people tend to take more funds out of the income stream as savings than they put back into the income stream as investments. Second, there is no necessary connection between an individual act of saving and an individual act of investment, so that changes in savings and in investment respectively can occur independently of one another. Third, the rigidity of costs makes it impossible for industry to adjust itself to falling money receipts without curtailing employment and the volume of production. Fourth, changes in the level of income lead to proportionately greater changes in the level of savings." Hardy, Comments, contained in Public Finance and Full Employment, Federal Reserve Board Postwar Economic Studies, No. 3, 136, at 138 (Dec. 1945).

[89] "[B]ut taxes must fall somewhere. If one tax is lowered, another must be raised to maintain revenue. Conceivably, we could impose a tax that would reduce neither consumption nor investment. The effect of such a tax would be merely to reduce hoarding, which occurs when income is neither spent nor invested in new plant, equipment, or other capital goods. But the kinds of taxes that would reduce the savings from which hoards are created are likely also to reduce the incentive for making investment. This presents a real dilemma." Blough, Problems of Postwar Federal Tax Policy, Nat'l Tax Ass'n, Proceedings of 37th National Conference (1944), 154–156. Specialized taxes discriminating in favor of investment and against hoarding have been proposed in this connection. Musgrave, Federal Tax Reform, in Public Finance and Full Employment, Federal Reserve System, Post War Economic Studies No. 3, at 41–43 (1945).

While stagnation may no longer be regarded as a serious problem, drastic shifts in the level of economic activity are still a matter for real concern. The above solution to what was conceived as the permanent problem of stagnation came to be adapted to another problem, that of hastening recovery from temporary depressions.[90] To the extent the government was to cover its expenditures by taxes, the case for progression again was that, as compared to other tax patterns, it best upheld the propensity of the society to consume. And just as the progressive tax was thought to be the appropriate tax in a period of decline, a regressive tax was thought to be the best vehicle for raising a given amount of revenue during a boom. More than any tax alternative the regressive tax would hold down consumption expenditures.

The merits of progression in the framework of such a program are not altogether the same as when progression is offered as a remedy for stagnation. In the depression context the proposal again relies on the assumptions that shifting income from the more to the less wealthy will increase the overall propensity to consume and that it will not impair the amount of investment. As to the latter assumption there is still the same question of how much the progressive rates will retard investment by dampening the incentives to take risks. But the former assumption encounters a new difficulty: in the short run it is by no means as plausible that a redistribution of income will increase the amount of consumption expenditure. The impact of the redistribution on consumption is subject to at least two significant offsets. While it may be improbable that the more wealthy will in the aggregate reduce their consumption expenditures by the full amount of the redistribution, it is certainly likely that there will be some reduction in the total amount of their spending. Perhaps more important is the impact on so-called negative savings. In depressed times the less wealthy dis-save by spending more than their incomes through borrowing or drawing on their accumulations. If their incomes are increased by a reduction in their tax burden, it is likely that some part of the increase will be used simply to reduce negative savings. To this extent the addition to their incomes will not be reflected in an increase in their expenditures. These two factors taken together render the net impact of the redistribution on the average propensity to consume highly obscure, and may obliterate it altogether.

However significant may be the objective of increasing consumption in a depression, the significance of the role of progression in achieving it

[90] Hansen, Fiscal Policy and Business Cycles (1941); Hansen, Stability and Expansion, in Twentieth Century Fund: Financing American Prosperity 206–26 (1945).

would seem to be slight. Nor is it clear that even if its impact were considerable it would be an indispensable method of enhancing consumption. The alternative to using progression to effect a reduction in taxes for some, at the expense of increasing taxes for others, is simply to reduce taxes uniformly for all without lowering government expenditures. Such a move would be equally or more effective in stimulating consumption, but it would be at the price of an increase in the government deficit. One's appraisal of this case for progression necessarily will reflect the degree of one's anxiety about increasing government deficits.

The final and decisive weakness of such a case for progression is that it is a part time case. There is a defense only when depression conditions prevail. Under boom conditions there is an explicit rejection of progression. And in the stable economy which we hope to achieve the merits of progression become a matter of indifference.[91]

Another approach to progression in the context of economic activity has been concerned with its usefulness in minimizing economic instability in the future. The thesis in essence is that a more even distribution of income in the society, which can be brought about by progression, will tend to result in a more constant rate of spending and therefore of economic activity. On the one hand the point may be that the propensity of an individual to consume is likely to be more stable the lower his level of income. Below the minimum subsistence level an individual will continue to spend all of his income and save none of it. But as to persons over that level this proposition is subject to much the same uncertainties as predictions previously noted about the magnitude of the propensity to consume. We do not know what causes shifts in private spending, and there is little basis for making predictions as to the likelihood and size of such shifts under one

---

[91] "Those who advocate progressive taxes, because they curtail hoarding by curtailing saving, seem to take no account (1) of the need for minimizing monetary uncertainty through the establishment of definite rules of policy, (2) of the need for rigid economy in the kinds of devices for implementing those rules, or (3) of the need for sharp focusing of responsibility for observance of the rules. Moreover, such taxes, as a device for controlling the velocity of money, have the disadvantage of working only in one direction; at any rate, no one appears to advocate their reduction or abolition in boom times as a means for checking a movement of dishoarding!

"The advocates of these intriguing heresies appear to argue that we cannot afford prosperity because additional income promotes hoarding; but the paradox, however salable and entertaining, is intellectual rubbish. One means for reducing hoarding, to be sure, is to keep people very poor. The excuse for killing of the goose, however, is very lame. There is no need for restricting saving in order to restrict hoarding; appropriate monetary rules, implemented by mandatory changes in the quantity of money, can assure adequate (or excessive) spending by making the alternative cost of hoarding as high as may be necessary, and without any deliberate diversion of funds from would-be savers to the more profligate or necessitous. Thus . . . the case for progression is enormously stronger than any monetary considerations on which it might be rested; and those who seek to support it in this way only raise doubts about an otherwise strong position." Simons, Personal Income Taxation 23 n. 14 (1938).

pattern of income distribution in the long run as compared with another. On the other hand the point may be that the magnitude of consumer expenditures is likely to be more constant than investment expenditures. A society which has a negligible accumulation of capital and is virtually living from hand to mouth may well necessarily maintain an almost constant full employment. The point thus seems to reduce to a kind of perverse complaint about having achieved a large accumulation of capital. Entirely apart from whether the impact of redistribution on future stability can be traced, these lines of argument are incomplete. Certainly the significance of redistribution for stability purposes will vary considerably, and perhaps may disappear altogether, depending on what monetary and fiscal policies are pursued by the society.

The placing of progression in the context of the quest for economic stability may in the end somewhat corroborate a conviction as to its merits, but standing alone it can never be adequate to establish such a conviction. None of these proposals to justify progression amounts to more than a mild underwriting of it. Against this must be weighed the very considerable difference that progression makes in the tax burdens of some individuals. Moreover, it should be noted that for the most part the proposals explicitly rely on the fact that progression redistributes income in the direction of lessening economic inequalities. They therefore might be viewed as part of the general case for progression on equalitarian grounds, and in this sense they anticipate a substantial concern of the essay with equality.

8

The more traditional place to begin the affirmative case for progression is with the simple notion of estimating the benefits which the taxpayer purchases with taxes. No one regards taxes as a completely one-sided transfer. Since it is obvious that each taxpayer derives some benefits from the operation of government, the magnitude of such benefits suggests itself as a standard for distributing the tax burden. If it can be shown that the benefits increase as income increases, and that at some levels of income benefits increase more rapidly than income, a compelling justification for progression will have been established.[92]

[92] For an extensive review of benefit theory see Seligman, Progressive Taxation in Theory and Practice 150–229 (2d ed., 1908); also see Weston, Principles of Justice in Taxation in 17 Columbia University Studies in History, Economics and Public Law, 160–71 (1903). Hackett's article on The Constitutionality of the Graduated Income Tax, which was noted in the text, section 3 supra, is based on an acceptance of benefit theory. 25 Yale L.J. 427 (1916). Today almost every textbook on public finance pays its respects to benefit theory as a principle for allocating the overall tax burden but treats it as being only of historical or academic interest in this connection.

Undoubtedly there are many instances of good correlation between a tax paid and a benefit received. The clearest case is one in which the government could readily sell the particular service on the market, as it does with the postal service, but where instead it uses the procedure of taxing those who receive the benefit. The benefit principle of taxing also has unquestioned propriety in connection with at least some situations in which the taxpayer is not free to avoid the tax by declining the benefit.[93] But the central services of government today could hardly be placed on a cash and carry arrangement, nor could the value of these benefits to particular taxpayers be traced. It need merely be asked what groups would be called upon to pay for the enforcement of the antitrust laws or policing the income tax itself or the cost of maintaining the courts. The diffuseness of the benefits from government today is frequently offered as a summary reason for limiting the benefit test to those isolated situations in which a direct correlation between the tax payment and the benefit exists.[94]

This is too summary an objection. The relevant question is whether, granting that most benefits from government cannot be particularized and traced, it nevertheless can be held that such benefits as a whole vary in some fashion with income. A good deal less than perfect correlation between benefits and incomes would be sufficient for the theory.

One attempt to establish a rough general correlation proceeds by way of distinguishing between the services of government to persons and its services to property.[95] The services to persons are said to be alike for all individuals, while the services to property are said to increase with the amount of property owned. In a famous analogy the state is compared to an insurance company insofar as the state protects property;[96] the premium for protection increases as the amount of property covered is increased. But this approach to correlation simply does not work. The only services of government which seem to be correlated with the quantity of

[93] See for example, Simons, Personal Income Taxation 34 et seq. (1938). A further use of the benefit principle is as a guide to what taxes should be borne locally rather than nationally. See Cannan, Equity and Economy in Taxation, 11 Econ. J. 469 (1901).

[94] Edgeworth suggested that in the search for a principle of tax justice the primary problem is "to determine the distribution of those taxes which are applied to common purposes, the benefits whereof cannot be allocated to any particular classes of citizens"; and the secondary problem is "to determine the distribution of taxation, not being limited to that amount of which the benefit is indiscriminate . . ." II Edgeworth, Papers Relating to Political Economy 235 (1925); see also Sidgwick, Principles of Political Economy 560–64 (2d ed., 1887).

[95] Sometimes the theory is stated in terms of the *cost* of the government services performed for each citizen rather than in terms of the *benefits* received from such services. This refinement may avoid the need of measuring subjective benefits but it does little else for the theory.

[96] The originator of the analogy appears to be Thiers. See discussion in Seligman, Progressive Taxation in Theory and Practice 169 et seq. (2d ed., 1908).

property owned by an individual are the police, fire-fighting and military forces; and even as to these the correlation seems to be grossly inadequate. A military establishment adequate to protect persons would necessarily be large enough to protect property from exterior violence. To a somewhat lesser extent this is probably also true of internal police and fire-fighting establishments. Further, even granting that there is some additional benefit to property owners from both such establishments, it surely does not vary with the value of the property which is being protected. Especially is this true in a society in which a large portion of property is in the form of intangibles. And in any event, in the modern state the maintenance of police and fire-fighting forces is likely to be only a small fraction of the total services performed by government.[97]

Another approach is more ingenious. It is founded on a double assumption: first, that the well-being of men, while not caused by the government, is dependent upon it in that government is a necessary condition for its existence; second, that the only aspect of well-being which is measurable is wealth or income and that it is therefore appropriate to take either of these as an index of the benefits flowing from government. The most frequent use of this approach is to divide income into that portion which is indispensable for obtaining the bare necessities of life and into a surplus which allows one to enjoy a fuller life, and then to argue that the benefits of government come only with a surplus. In this form the argument leads to incorporating a minimum standard of living exemption in an otherwise flat tax and thus to producing the limited progression accompanying an exemption. The approach has also been used to justify more extensive progression by appearing to find the requisite correlation between the benefits of government and the amount of income.

[97] "[S]ome consistent adherents of the *quid pro quo* principle go on to observe, that protection being required for person as well as property, and everybody's person receiving the same amount of protection, a poll-tax of a fixed sum per head is a proper equivalent for this part of the benefits of government, while the remaining part, protection to property, should be paid for in proportion to property. There is in this adjustment a false air of nice adaptation, very acceptable to some minds. But in the first place, it is not admissible that the protection of persons and that of property are the sole purposes of government. The ends of government are as comprehensive as those of the social union. They consist of all the good, and all the immunity from evil, which the existence of government can be made either directly or indirectly to bestow. In the second place, the practice of setting definite values on things essentially indefinite, and making them a ground of practical conclusions, is peculiarly fertile in false views of social questions. . . . The same judges, soldiers, and sailors who protect the one protect the other, and the larger income does not necessarily, though it may sometimes, require even more policemen. Whether the labour and expense of the protection, or the feelings of the protected person, or any other definite thing be made the standard, there is no such proportion as the one supposed, nor any other definable proportion." Mill, Principles of Political Economy, 804–805 Bk. 5, c. II, On the General Principles of Taxation (Ashley's ed., 1923).

But this approach also runs into serious difficulties. It stretches the ordinary notion of benefit almost beyond recognition. In doing so it loses the strength it derived from the good sense of the simpler notion of particular benefits conferred by government on particular persons. And, even accepting the proposition that all benefits are to be credited to government, it is highly questionable whether wealth or income is an adequate index of total well-being. Other factors, such as health and longevity, are surely of importance, and we know enough about their distribution to be sure that they are not distributed in accordance with wealth or income.

As far as the affirmative case for progression is concerned, there is an overriding weakness to all of these benefit approaches. It is difficult, as has been pointed out, to show that greater benefits are received from government by people having greater incomes. But even if this proposition could be established convincingly, it would by no means establish the case for progression. For the principle of progression requires not merely that the benefits increase with income but that they increase more rapidly than income. If attention is directed to the costs of protecting property, it would be preposterous to assume that such costs increase more rapidly than the value of the property being protected. If attention is directed to the well-being derived from wealth or income, progression would require the even more heroic assumption that the benefits from money increase more rapidly than the amount of money and that therefore money has an increasing value or utility to its possessors.

There are still other difficulties. Where particular benefits are traceable, the use of the benefit principle in allocating tax burdens may be incompatible with other objectives of society. There clearly are some benefits conferred by the government which cannot, without defeating their very purpose, be made contingent on the ability of the recipient to pay for them. The most common instances today are education and welfare subsidies to the underprivileged. If it has been decided that the government should perform these services, it must also have been decided that to this extent the benefit principle is to be subordinated. Assuming that the welfare decision was made deliberately, its incompatibility with the benefit principle tells nothing about the wisdom of the decision.

There remains the question whether, if the benefit analysis does not supply a case for progression, it necessarily provides a persuasive case for proportion. Indeed, historically almost all exponents of benefit theory employed it to support proportion as against progression. There is the well worn rhetorical question: Since the rich and the poor pay at the same rate for bread, why shouldn't they pay at the same rate in buying government?

However, it is easily seen that the shortcomings of benefit theory are almost as embarrassing to the case for proportion as that for progression. In either case the difficulties of isolating and measuring particular benefits are for the most part insurmountable. If, as a result, resort is had to some general assumption about the distribution of the highly diffuse benefits of government, the most plausible one is that all citizens benefit approximately alike.[98] The logical outcome of the benefit test would then be a highly regressive tax system.

For any attempt to apply the benefit principle generally as a standard in allocating taxes, an appropriate epitaph can be found in a comment by John Stuart Mill: to assert that individuals receive significantly different benefits from living in a particular society is in effect to assert that there is something seriously wrong with that society.[99]

9

Another major line of justification for progression looks not at the benefits which taxpayers receive from government but rather at the sacrifices which the payment of taxes entails. This approach builds on the undeniably true observation that the payment of taxes represents a coerced contribution to the government. It ignores the benefits received from government and treats taxes as though they were a confiscation of property. The problem then becomes one of confiscating in an equitable manner.[100]

On this foundation it initially seems possible to construct a sound argument for progression. An equitable apportioning of sacrifice requires in-

[98] "If we wanted to estimate the degrees of benefit which different persons derive from the protection of government we should have to consider who would suffer most if that protection were withdrawn: to which question if any answer could be made, it must be that those would suffer most who were weakest in mind or body, either by nature or by position. Indeed, such persons would almost infallibly be slaves. If there were any justice, therefore, in the theory of justice now under consideration, those who are least capable of helping or defending themselves, being those to whom the protection of government is the most indispensable, ought to pay the greatest share of its price: the reverse of the true idea of distributive justice, which consists not in imitating but in redressing the inequalities and wrongs of nature." Ibid., at 805.

[99] "Government must be regarded as so pre-eminently a concern of all, that to determine who are most interested in it is of no real importance. If a person or class of persons receive so small a share of the benefit as makes it necessary to raise the question, there is something else than taxation which is amiss, and the thing to be done is to remedy the defect, instead of recognising it and making it a ground for demanding less taxes." Ibid., at 806.

[100] Sacrifice theory does not require the complete rejection of the benefit criterion. Sacrifice notions come into play to the extent that benefits are not directly traceable or to the extent that traceable benefits are a consequence of deliberate welfare measures and are received by those not intended to pay for them. See text, section 22 infra. Where benefits are directly traceable and are not the result of welfare measures there is complete compatibility between the benefit and sacrifice criteria since in these cases there is no sacrifice involved in the payment of the tax. See Sidgwick, Principles of Political Economy 566 (2d ed., 1887).

flicting equal hurt on each taxpayer.[101] It seems likely that a dollar has less "value" for a person with a million dollars of income than for a person with only a thousand dollars of income. To take the same number of dollars from each is not to require the same amount of sacrifice from them. Instead a fair tax would take more from the wealthier individual, and this is what a progressive tax does.

This sort of sacrifice analysis has been the most prominent form of argument for progression both at a popular and at a sophisticated level. Sacrifice doctrine has been subjected to an extraordinary amount of analysis. Although the doctrine is not as fashionable as it was a generation ago, formidable authority can still be cited for it.[102] While some of the refinements of the analysis have been tempting targets for ridicule, the doctrine as a whole makes up a curious and fascinating chapter of intellectual history. In fact, by far the largest part of the intellectual history of progression theory has been the development of sacrifice doctrine. Moreover, whatever the history, there is a strong popular feeling today which apparently supports progression on the basis of sacrifice notions. It is therefore worthwhile to be patient with the analysis of it.

The analysis can best begin with a consideration of what sacrifice means. While the doctrine ultimately refers to the pleasures of having money and the pains of paying taxes, it need not commit itself to an exploration of the actual subjective mental states of each individual taxpayer. Rather, in a fashion reminiscent of the law's use of the reasonable man standard, the doctrine seeks to abstract out individual differences and to make assumptions about the reactions to money that men have in common. The assumptions are, first, that the only significant variable in men's taste for money is the amount of money they have; and, second, that men's appetite for money declines as the amount of money which they have increases. A convenient shorthand for these assumptions is to say

[101] It is customary, in sacrifice analysis, to treat all money taken from a person in taxes as inflicting sacrifice or hurt; and this usage is followed here. But it has sometimes been urged that once a person has become accustomed to a certain rate of tax the payment of that rate no longer involves a hurt since he does not regard the tax money as ever having been part of his income. "One might almost as well describe the difference between our present happiness and that what we might enjoy in Paradise as being a 'hurt.'" Stamp, Fundamental Principles of Taxation 50 (1921). There is a core of truth here; and it does raise the problem of the advisability of ever basically changing tax rates or tax patterns. But if carried too far it not only eliminates concern with sacrifice theory but any concern with ultimate justice in taxation.

[102] In recent years such economists as Pigou, Fisher, Harrod, and Lerner have subscribed to it in some form, and Dalton treats it with considerable respect.

"The quantitative relation of well-being to income, and interpersonal comparisons as well, are generally accepted as having enough stability to justify highly progressive taxation, even in face of a likelihood that production will be reduced." Knight, Introduction to Menger Principles of Economics 19 (Dingwall and Hoselitz trans. 1950).

there is a general utility curve for money which has a downward slope. It appears not to matter whether the curve is regarded as descriptive of a given individual when money is added to or subtracted from his total, or as descriptive of two or more individuals who have different amounts of money. Furthermore, the image of such a curve is convenient in that it apparently can be used to call attention to both the aggregate amount of utility of a given total of money or to its marginal utility, meaning the utility of the last dollar added to a given total.[103] These add up to a considerable set of assumptions which will be scrutinized closely later. It will be useful however to accept the assumptions for the moment and see whether they lead to progression.

If a general utility curve for money is taken as available to measure the sacrifice involved in paying taxes, the next step in the argument seems easy. At first impression it appears axiomatic that sacrifices for taxes should be be exacted of all citizens equally. But "equality of sacrifice" is ambiguous, and its two meanings may yield radically different results in dictating a scale of taxes. It can mean that the quantity of sacrifice, that is, the loss of units of utility, demanded of each individual be equal ("*equal sacrifice*"), or it can mean that each should be required to give up an equal percentage of his total utility derived from money ("*proportionate sacrifice*").[104]

To complete the argument for progression on grounds of equality of sacrifice two further inquiries are required. The first is whether under either of these sacrifice standards *any* declining utility curve for money will dictate progression or whether the steepness of decline has to be specified to some extent. This is an important step since it is one thing to assume that the utility of money declines but quite another to assume the rate at which it declines. Clearly, the fewer the demands the argument makes on knowledge of the slope of the curve, the stronger the argument will be. The second inquiry is whether the two sacrifice standards have

[103] For present purposes the curve is taken to cover only income above the minimum subsistence level. It is frequently said that income below the subsistence level has infinite utility. The propriety of excluding such income from the curve is discussed at length in Cohen-Stuart, A Contribution to the Theory of the Progressive Income Tax (1889) (Ms. trans., Te Velde, University of Chicago Libraries, 1936) 53–60.

[104] In Edgeworth's words, "The honour of clearly distinguishing these principles appears to belong to Mr. Cohen-Stuart." II Edgeworth, Papers Relating to Political Economy 107 n. 6 (1925). He goes on to take Seligman to task for saying that there was no significance to the distinction and that everyone had always meant proportionate sacrifice in using the term "equality of sacrifice." Ibid., at 235–37. There is no doubt that the Cohen-Stuart essay is the ablest presentation of the proportionate sacrifice thesis. The essay is also valuable in that it contains careful discussions of several continental writers on progression whose works do not appear to have been translated. A concise summary of the operation of the sacrifice formulas is found in Dalton, Public Finance c. IX (15th ed., 1946).

equal appeal. If they do, the argument may be seriously embarrassed by the difficulty of choosing between them since they produce quite different results when applied to any given utility curve.

It is somewhat surprising to discover that the equal sacrifice standard applied to a declining utility curve does not inevitably result in progression in tax rates.[105] In fact it may result in a regressive scale of rates. This can be seen by first assuming that the utility curve does not decline and that all dollars have an equal amount of utility to a person regardless of the total dollars he has. Equal sacrifice would then mean that each person paid the same number of dollars of tax regardless of the amount of his income. The tax would obviously be regressive; a person with twice as much income as another would pay an effective rate of tax one half that paid by the other. In order to have each pay the same rate of tax the man with twice the income must be required to pay twice the number of dollars in tax. For these unequal dollar payments to exact equal sacrifices from the two taxpayers, the utility of the dollars paid out by the more opulent must be half that of the dollars paid out by the other; and likewise if one person has ten times the income of another, equal sacrifice under a proportionate tax will be achieved only if the utilities of the dollars taken from them are in the ratio of one to ten. To generalize, in order for equal sacrifice to result in a proportionate tax the utility curve for money must be such that for any given percentage increase in the amount of money there must be a like percentage decrease in the marginal utility of that money.[106]

For convenience in designating this possible relation of income and utility, we shall refer to such a curve as a rectangular hyperbola. Any less steep curve would result in a regressive tax under equal sacrifice. Thus to get progression from the equal sacrifice standard requires not

---

[105] "Though the ground is now fully prepared, it will be convenient to pause for a moment before attempting a constructive argument, in order to clear away a false opinion which appears to be somewhat widely entertained. This opinion is to the effect that, in all circumstances, in order to secure equal sacrifice, the tax formula must be, in some measure, *progressive*, in the sense that the rate of taxation per £ of income grows as incomes grow. This proposition is supposed to be logically deducible from the law of diminishing utility. That supposition is incorrect. All that the law of diminishing utility asserts is that the last £1 of a £1000 income carries less satisfaction than the last £1 of a £100 income does. From this datum it cannot be inferred that, in order to secure equal sacrifice . . . taxation must be progressive. In order to prove that the principle of equal sacrifice necessarily involves progression we should need to know that the last £10 of a £1000 income carry less satisfaction than the last £1 of a £100 income; and this the law of diminishing utility does not assert." Pigou, A Study in Public Finance 85–86 (3d rev. ed., 1951).

[106] Other ways of describing such a curve are Edgeworth's, "that utility diminishes in inverse ratio to means," II Edgeworth, Papers Relating to Political Economy 107 (1925); and Marshall's, "that the increased happiness which he derives from the addition of one per cent to his income is the same whatever his income be." Marshall, Principles of Economics, Mathematical Appendix 842 n. VIII (8th ed., 1925).

only that the utility of money does decline but that it declines more rapidly than a rectangular hyperbola.[107]

The proportionate sacrifice standard would clearly result in progression with any utility curve that would satisfy the requirements for progression under equal sacrifice; and obviously it would also do so under some less steep curves as well. Indeed it would seem to do so for any money utility curve which declines at all. This appears to follow from the observation that if money had a constant utility, the proportionate sacrifice standard would result in a proportionate tax. To impose the same percentage of sacrifice on all taxpayers would then simply require taking the same percentage of dollars from each of them. Therefore, it might seem that, no matter how gentle the slope of a declining utility curve, it would be sufficient under the proportionate sacrifice standard to produce something more than a proportionate tax and thus to produce some degree of progression. Over sixty years ago, however, the error of this reasoning was discovered by a Dutch economist, Cohen-Stuart, who elaborately analyzed the consequences under the proportionate sacrifice standard of various utility curves for money. He demonstrated that it is possible to construct utility curves which declined in such a fashion that, on some parts of the curves, a regressive tax followed from application of the proportionate sacrifice standard.[108] While it seems that proportionate sacrifice would result in progression under most curves that could be postulated,[109] any argument for progression based on that standard loses some of its force because of the fact that a declining curve does not always result in progression.

The choice between the equal sacrifice and the proportionate sacrifice criteria, although seldom discussed in the literature, does not seem overly difficult when further analyzed.[110] Any theory of equalizing the sacrifice of

[107] See, for example, Pigou, A Study in Public Finance 89 (3d rev. ed., 1951).

[108] Cohen-Stuart, A Contribution to the Theory of the Progressive Income Tax (1889) (Ms. trans., Te Velde, University of Chicago Libraries, 1936) 116–37. The tables developed by Cohen-Stuart to demonstrate his point are reproduced in Seligman, Progressive Taxation in Theory and Practice 218–22 (2d ed., 1909). The point is also made by Edgeworth in II Papers Relating to Political Economy 239–40 (1925).

[109] Cohen-Stuart and Edgeworth confine themselves to showing only that it is *possible* to find an instance of a declining utility curve which would not result in progression under the equal sacrifice formula. Neither suggests that such a curve is at all plausible. It takes considerable ingenuity to find such an instance, and the curve is eccentric.

[110] The history of the proportionate sacrifice idea has been curious. The distinction between proportionate sacrifice and equal sacrifice was repeatedly lost even after it had been painstakingly pointed out. Seligman did not take the distinction seriously. See note 104 supra. Weston likewise blurred the distinction. Principles of Justice in Taxation, 17 Columbia University Studies in History, Economy and Public Law 204–205 (1903). A good recent example of a

taxpayers implicitly assumes that the taxes are a necessary evil falling upon a distribution of money, and therefore upon a distribution of satisfactions, which is otherwise acceptable. With this assumption the problem is not to use the tax system to adjust existing inequalities in that distribution but simply to leave all taxpayers equally "worse off" after taxes. The vice of the equal sacrifice formula is that it is regressive when measured by satisfactions and this becomes compellingly clear if large enough sacrifices are exacted equally from each taxpayer.[111] The corresponding virtue of the proportionate sacrifice formula is that it remains neutral as to the relative distribution of satisfactions among taxpayers. Under it they are all equally "worse off" after taxes.[112]

The primary case for some progression, then, in terms of equality of sacrifice is the case under the proportionate sacrifice formula.[113] As a principle of justice it is intuitively attractive; it makes relatively few demands on knowledge about the utility curve for money, other than that it

refusal to take this distinction seriously is found in Taylor, Economics of Public Finance, 293, particularly note 13 (1948).

Although Seligman insisted that proportionate sacrifice always was meant by those talking about equality of sacrifice, it is not clear that he himself always maintained that meaning. It is quite clear that most subsequent discussion of equality of sacrifice has been concerned with the equal sacrifice, and not the proportionate sacrifice, formula. Pigou, while clearly recognizing the distinction, has an elaborate discussion of equal sacrifice but merely mentions proportionate sacrifice in passing. Harrod's effort to buttress the case for progressive taxation on grounds of equality of sacrifice was concerned exclusively with the requirements of the utility curve under the equal sacrifice formula. See text, section 10. Fagan, although aware of the distinction, in an extensive criticism of sacrifice theory appears to have been talking only about equal sacrifice. Recent and Contemporary Theories of Progressive Taxation, 46 J. Pol. Econ. 457 (1938). Simons in effect disposed of proportionate sacrifice with an exclamation mark. Simons, Personal Income Taxation 6 (1938).

[111] Pigou suggests the limiting case is that in which the amount of revenue to be raised is such that the sacrifice imposed on the wealthy man is more than the total satisfactions available to the less wealthy man before tax. Here equal sacrifice requires taking all of the poor man's income. Pigou, A Study in Public Finance 84 (3d rev. ed., 1951).

[112] The exemption of income under the minimum subsistence level poses a minor problem of consistency for both the equal and proportionate sacrifice formulas. Equalizing of sacrifices appears to imply that everyone who has any income at all should make some sacrifice, however small. But see note 103 supra.

[113] It is undoubtedly late in the day to sound disturbed over the fate of proportionate sacrifice as a refinement of equal sacrifice. Nevertheless, proportionate sacrifice is not only the most defensible version of the equality of sacrifice notion but it turns out to be the most defensible version of sacrifice analysis in any form. (See discussion of minimum sacrifice in the text, section 11 infra). So long as sacrifice ideas retain such popular vitality it is worth-while examining them carefully, and this means assessing the proportionate sacrifice formula. There are, as indicated in the text, section 12 infra, some crucial general objections to any analysis based on sacrifice doctrine, and it may be possible to dispose of sacrifice doctrine on these more general grounds without examining the particular refinements of sacrifice theory. However, it would seem that only by appreciating the strength of the case for proportionate sacrifice can one reach a tested conviction as to the ultimate weakness of sacrifice analysis.

declines; and it narrows considerably the issue between progressive and proportionate taxation. As between one who favors proportional taxation on grounds of its neutrality and one who favors the proportionate sacrifice standard on grounds of its neutrality there is only the issue of whether there is a meaningful and sufficiently ascertainable money utility curve for all taxpayers. From one point of view proportionate sacrifice represents a more ambitious, if less practical, attempt to achieve neutrality in the collection of taxes.[114]

10

It has been shown that to produce some progression the proportionate sacrifice standard, under most possible utility curves for money, requires no knowledge of the curve other than that it declines somewhat. But even assuming that it is meaningful to talk about a declining utility curve for money, the case for progression on grounds of equality of sacrifice is not free of difficulties. The steeper the utility curve, the steeper will be the progression dictated by proportionate sacrifice. Wide variations in the utility curve are compatible with the general assumption that it declines; and it follows that wide variations in the patterns of tax rates are all possible unless some further knowledge about the slope of the utility curve is accessible.

This difficulty of identifying the "proper" rate pattern from among the great variety of patterns all of which are progressive was given its most famous expression over a hundred years ago by McCulloch. "The moment," he said, "you abandon . . . the cardinal principle of exacting from all individuals the same proportion of their income or their property, you are at sea without rudder or compass, and there is no amount of injustice or folly you may not commit."[115] Every proponent of progression has had

[114] See Cohen-Stuart, A Contribution to the Theory of the Progressive Income Tax (1889) (Ms. trans., Te Velde, University of Chicago Libraries, 1936).

[115] McCulloch, Taxation and the Funding System 142 (1845). This is probably the most quoted passage in the literature on progressive taxation. The specter of progressive taxation moved McCulloch to eloquence at this point:
"The reasons that made the step be taken in the first instance, backed as they are sure to be by agitation and clamour, will impel you forwards. Having once given way, having said that a man with 500 £. a-year shall pay 5 per cent., another with 1000 £. 10 per cent., and another with 2000 £. 20 per cent., on what pretence or principle can you stop in your ascending scale? Why not take 50 per cent. from the man of 2000 £. a-year, and confiscate all the higher class of incomes before you tax the lower? In such matters the maxim of *obsta principiis* should be firmly adhered to by every prudent and honest statesman. Graduation is not an evil to be paltered with. Adopt it and you will effectually paralyse industry and check accumulation; at the same time that every man who has any property will hasten, by carrying it out of the country, to protect it from confiscation. The savages described by Montesquieu, who to get at the fruit cut down the tree, are about as good financiers as the advocates of this

to make his peace with this metaphor. Probably the best known rejoinder is that of Professor Seligman, a half century later. "It is true that proportion is in one sense certain," replied Professor Seligman, "and that progression is uncertain. The argument, however, proves too much. An uncertain rate, if it be in the general direction of justice, may nevertheless be preferable to a rate which, like that of proportion, may be more certain without being so equitable."[116]

But if the argument does prove too much the rejoinder does not prove enough. There are two grounds for thinking that the rejoinder is too optimistic in its calculus of the relative chance of justice under progression as compared with proportion. First, it is possible for two progressive rate scales to differ more radically between themselves than the less progressive scale differs from proportion. Accordingly it is at least possible to have a progressive rate pattern which, judged by such a standard as equality of sacrifice, is more unfair than is a proportionate tax. Second, any injustice from having a proportionate tax would be in the form of having the many pay a little more tax than justice would require. In contrast the injustice of an "improper" scale of progression would be in the form of having the few pay considerably more in taxes than justice would require. Thus, unless more is known about how to select a just scale of progressive rates, it is rash to assume that the certain injustice of proportion is likely to be greater than the uncertain injustice of progression.

The selection of a just scale of progressive rates under the proportionate sacrifice standard thus requires more knowledge about the utility of money than the mere fact that it declines.[117] Perhaps the most bizarre chapter in the intellectual history of progression consists in the many attempts to state the shape of the curve.

While the possible range of declining utility curves is enormous, the methods of deriving such a curve are few. The most common approach has been to examine the matter introspectively and attempt to embody the conclusions in a mathematical formula. Any formula for this purpose, as a practical matter, has to be simple enough to be carried in the mind easily. This probably explains the fact that the most popular guess has

---

sort of taxes. Wherever they are introduced security is at an end. Even if taxes on income were otherwise the most unexceptionable, the adoption of the principle of graduation would make them about the very worst that could be devised."

[116] Seligman, Progressive Taxation in Theory and Practice 294 (2d ed., 1908). The same type of rejoinder was made by Taussig. "The same difficulty might be urged against all sorts of movements for reform. Few except the out-and-out socialists have clear notions of their ultimate goal. But it suffices for the average man to know in what direction he is moving." II Principles of Economics 488 (1911).

[117] This is all the more true of the equal sacrifice formula.

been that the curve is a rectangular hyperbola, which requires merely that a given percentage of total satisfactions taken away affects a man in the same degree regardless of the amount of income he has.[118] For obvious reasons even its friends have been reluctant to say more in behalf of this curve than that it is "not unplausible."[119]

The guess about the rectangular hyperbola has also furnished a convenient measuring stick, and those who have thought that the curve was otherwise have usually confined themselves to urging that the proper curve fell on the progressive or regressive side of the rectangular hyperbola. The most notable recent effort to show that the proper curve is more progressive is that of A. C. Pigou.[120] In essence he argues that at high levels of income the satisfactions derived from additional income are in large measure based on comparing one's income with that of one's economic or social rivals. Therefore, he concludes, even if large shares of income are taken away from all members of this wealthy class, there will be little loss of satisfaction to any of its members since the satisfaction based on invidious comparison is not likely to be substantially diminished. This is perhaps the most persuasive presentation of the case for a steeply declining utility curve inasmuch as it refers to data which seem to be somewhat accessible to common observation and which have been noted independently in other connections.[121] But, since all that is in issue at the moment is whether the curve is as steep as Pigou urges, it is possible to cast doubt on his conclusion. Insofar as the point depends on competitive consumption of the wealthy, it does not take into account that part of their money which is not devoted to personal consumption. The personal asceticism of Henry Ford and John D. Rockefeller is legendary. Moreover, it is by no means clear that conspicuous consumption is a talent restricted to the upper income classes. Much contemporary mass advertising is high testimony in behalf of the opposite assumption.

Another attempt to show that the curve declines more steeply than a rectangular hyperbola deserves some comment. In a short note Roy Harrod has suggested that perhaps one can get at the intensity with which people value varying amounts of money by considering the amount of effort they are willing to put forth to earn money.[122] The heart of his thesis

---

[118] This hypothesis is credited to Bernoulli. See note 106 supra.

[119] Pigou, A Study in Public Finance 90 (3d rev. ed., 1951).

[120] Ibid., at 91.

[121] See for example, Veblen, Theory of the Leisure Class (1899).

[122] Harrod, Progressive Taxation and Equal Sacrifice, 40 Econ. J. 704 (1930); there is an extended discussion of the Harrod note in Fagan, Recent and Contemporary Theories of Progressive Taxation, 46 J. Pol. Econ. 457, 468–75 (1938).

is that if, all other things being equal, everybody has the same disinclination to work, that is, to put forth effort, then the utility of income to men might be priced in terms of units of effort. If it can be shown that the amount of effort that another prospective dollar will call forth decreases as the amount of a man's income increases, one explanation of this may be that the more dollars a man has the less he values the next dollar. Assuming this to be the correct explanation, it would establish only that the utility of money declines somewhat. The only purpose of Harrod's analysis, however, is to show that it declines more steeply than a rectangular hyperbola. To do this he goes to the hypothetical case of all men being willing to work the same total amount regardless of their rate of pay and points out that under those circumstances the effort-income curve would be a rectangular hyperbola. This must be the case because total effort is taken to be a constant regardless of income, and therefore the willingness to expend effort varies inversely with the rate of pay and hence with total income. It then remains only to question how closely the hypothetical case corresponds to the facts. This Harrod does by pointing out that at the minimum subsistence level it probably is true that men will put out a maximum effort regardless of their remuneration and that at some level of great wealth men will refuse to perform any work regardless of the compensation offered. Connecting up these two extreme points necessarily results in a curve steeper than a rectangular hyperbola.

Confining discussion at present to the distinctive thesis which Harrod sets out to demonstrate, it is extremely doubtful that he succeeds.[123] His critical step is establishing the rectangular hyperbola as the measuring stick, and this is done by positing the case in which all men as a matter of choice will work only a given amount and no more regardless of their rates of pay. This is necessarily an unreal case for Harrod since the rest of his analysis turns on showing that in the real world men act otherwise. In effect the hypothetical case embarks one on the interesting venture of explaining what would motivate men if they acted differently than they in fact do act. But waiving this difficulty, the more serious obstacle is Harrod's explanation of motivation in his hypothetical case. If men were always to work the same amount regardless of their incomes, would not this afford the most compelling evidence that we knew nothing about the relationship between income and effort? In any event it would seem far more plausible to assume that under the posited circumstances men were not motivated by income at all but performed work without concerning them-

---

[123] There are good reasons for doubting whether the effort price of income is in the end of any use in establishing a utility curve. See text, section 12 infra.

selves with rewards. Thus Harrod seems to fall short of establishing that his effort-income curve is at least a rectangular hyperbola and therefore does not succeed in proving that that curve—or the money utility curve which he hoped to derive from it—is even steeper.

All in all the attempts to discover more about the utility curve than the fact that it declines somewhat are interesting but not persuasive.[124] With not too much risk of overstatement, it can be said that only by intuition can the general shape of a curve be derived, and intuition is of dubious reliability when it comes to setting exact rates of tax.

II

Up to this point the case for progression on grounds of sacrifice has been keyed to some notion of exacting equality of sacrifice from taxpayers. There is however another main line of sacrifice theory which appeals to a wholly different standard. It has an easily traced intellectual history running from Bentham and Mill to Edgeworth and Pigou, and it appears to have enlisted some of the best minds which have studied the problem of progression.[125] It seeks to apply directly to taxation the utilitarian first

[124] Two further approaches should be noted. Fisher outlined a prospectus for deriving the utility curve empirically by studying what it is that people buy with their incomes under different price structures. His apparatus for isolating the relevant data from the budgets of similar families in different communities was elaborate. He cautiously suggested that his rough preliminary use of the method tended to justify the adoption of progressive taxation; but he did not indicate which of the sacrifice criteria he was employing. Fisher, A Statistical Method for Measuring "Marginal Utility" and Testing the Justice of a Progressive Income Tax, in Economic Essays Contributed in Honor of John Bates Clark 157–93 (1927). The article is criticized at length in Fagan, Recent and Contemporary Theories of Progressive Taxation, 46 J. Pol. Econ. 457, 475–80 (1938). It does not appear that Fisher's method, whatever the empirical difficulties, escapes from the difficulties entailed in making the basic assumptions which appear to be required for any money utility analysis. See text, section 12 infra. Cf. Robbins, An Essay on the Nature and Significance of Economic Science, 141 n. 1 (2d ed., 1935). Pigou gives the Fisher method a nod of approval in A Study in Public Finance 92 (3d rev. ed., 1951). One attempt to apply the Fisher method is found in Frisch, New Methods of Measuring Marginal Utility (1932). Fagan also criticizes Frisch, supra this note at 480–85. Confidence in the ability of future empiricists to find the utility curve has been expressed recently in Preinreich, The Theory of Progressive Taxation, 25 Taxes 742 (1947).

The other approach is that of Cohen-Stuart, who in effect attempted to estimate the margin of error involved in basing a progressive tax on a utility curve in the shape of a rectangular hyperbola. He posited two curves, one with a steep slope and the other with a mild slope, such that it seemed probable to him that the true curve would fall somewhere between these two extremes. He then computed the tax rates under the three curves under the proportionate sacrifice formula and showed that the deviation of the rates based on the rectangular hyperbola from the rates based on the other two curves was considerably less than the deviations between the curves themselves. He concluded that the chance of error in the rates, if a rectangular hyperbola is taken as the utility curve for money, is not disturbing. Cohen-Stuart, A Contribution to the Theory of the Progressive Income Tax (1889) (Ms. trans., Te Velde, University of Chicago Libraries, 1936) 192 et seq.

[125] Bentham is the ultimate forbearer of the minimum sacrifice theory. Sidgwick, in a significant discussion, points out that the prima facie case for greater economic equality on

principle that law should be designed to bring about the greatest good for
the greatest number, or more precisely, the greatest quantity of total
satisfaction.[126] In taxation this would require taxing so as to keep to a
minimum the aggregate sacrifice imposed on the community as a whole.

It might at first impression be thought that the two sacrifice principles,
although based on different theories, would always yield the same result;
that is, that equality of sacrifice would always result in minimum sacrifice.
And in fact in a passage which his followers have ever since been busy
explaining, Mill seems to have so concluded. "Whatever sacrifices it [a
government] requires from them," he said, "should be made to bear as
nearly as possible with the same pressure upon all, which, it must be observed, is the mode by which least sacrifice is occasioned on the whole."[127]

utilitarian grounds follows from two propositions of Bentham: that increased wealth brings
increased satisfaction and that increases in wealth increase satisfactions in a declining ratio.
Sidgwick discusses these propositions in connection with the optimum distribution of wealth
but concludes that it is unwise for the society to attempt to redistribute wealth. Hence he
did not favor using taxation as a means to greater equality. Sidgwick, Principles of Political
Economy 518–33, 566–71 (2d ed., 1887).

In his essay, The Ethical Basis of Distribution and Its Application to Taxation, 6 Annals
79–99 (1895), Carver examines the justice of the distribution of economic goods with a view
to determining justice in taxation, and in so doing makes the first explicit statement of the
minimum sacrifice principle. The principle is elaborated by him in a second essay, The Minimum Sacrifice Theory of Taxation, 19 Pol. Sci. Q. 66 (1904).

Edgeworth restates and refines the principle rigorously in two essays, The Pure Theory
of Taxation, written in 1897, and Minimum Sacrifice versus Equal Sacrifice, written in 1910.
II Papers Relating to Political Economy 63, 100–125, 234 (1925).

The final elaboration of the principle is made by Pigou. The latest statement of his
position is found in A Study in Public Finance (3d rev. ed., 1951).

The role of Mill in the development of the principle is odd indeed. See notes 127–28 infra.

Undoubtedly the development of marginal utility analysis by Jevons was an almost indispensable step for the explicit statement of minimum sacrifice as a principle of taxation.

[126] "The popular, as compared with the exact, formula has only one disadvantage; that it is
nonsense." II Edgeworth, Papers Relating to Political Economy 241 (1925).

[127] Mill, Principles of Political Economy 804 (Ashley's ed., 1923). Virtually all discussions
of sacrifice theory start with this passage from Mill. It seems likely that this is the first reference to equal sacrifice as a principle of taxation. But it has also served as a starting point for
discussions of minimum sacrifice. Although Mill appears nominally to espouse both the principle of equal sacrifice and the principle of minimum sacrifice, he can scarcely be charged with
adhering to either principle as subsequently developed since he refused to rely on notions
of the declining utility of money.

There are some suggestions prior to Mill that taxation ought to take into account the
probability that money has declining utility. The position of Adam Smith is at least as ambiguous as that of Mill. While he said "the subjects of every state ought to contribute toward the
support of government, as nearly as possible in proportion to their respective abilities, that is,
in proportion to the revenue which they respectively enjoy under the protection of the state,"
Smith, IV Wealth of Nations c. 2 (1776); he also stated: "It is not very unreasonable that the
rich should contribute to the public expense, not only in proportion to their revenue, but something more in proportion." V Wealth of Nations c. 2, pt. 2 (1776). Say, in his work on political
economy written in 1803, argues that "if it be desired to tax individual income, in such manner
as to press lighter in proportion as that income approaches to the confines of bare necessity,

To this day there remains a nice question as to just what Mill himself may have meant,[128] but there is no question that if the utility of money declines at all, equal sacrifice and minimum sacrifice always yield different results.

Assuming a dollar is worth less to the man with the larger income than to the man with the smaller income, a dollar taken from the former will involve less sacrifice than one taken from the latter. If the state were to take only two dollars in all, the minimum sacrifice formula would require that both dollars be taken from the man with the larger income. This necessarily follows since after the first dollar is taken from the wealthier man, his income will still be larger than that of the other; therefore, taking the second dollar from him will occasion less sacrifice than taking a dollar from the less wealthy man.[129] The logic of this simple example would seem to extend to taking the third, the fourth and even the ten thousandth dollar in tax all from the wealthier man so long as he still remained the wealthier of the two men.[130] In the words of Pigou, the system if fully carried out would require

lopping off the tops of all incomes above the minimum income and leaving everybody, after taxation, with equal incomes. If the amount of revenue required is not enough to absorb the whole of the surpluses above the minimum . . . the logical procedure would be first to take for the government's needs the tops of the highest incomes, and then to continue taxing middle grade incomes and giving bounties from the proceeds

---

taxation must not only be equitably apportioned, but must press on revenue with progressive gravity." Quoted in Bullock, Selected Readings in Public Finance 235 (2d ed., 1920). It is Say's remarks which moved McCulloch to his burst of eloquence against progressive taxes. See note 115 supra.

[128] An amusing study could be written on the many efforts of those who came after Mill to save him from error in this passage. Our contribution to this tradition runs as follows: Mill did not make the error he is usually accused of making; that is, that the equal sacrifice and the minimum sacrifice principles always give the same results. He could not have made this error since in this same passage he found the declining utility of money to be "too disputable altogether." This error cannot arise unless one assumes that money has declining utility. Nor is his conclusion about "least sacrifice on the whole" nonsense without such an assumption. It is true that if money has constant utility, the loss of utility to the person overtaxed will be exactly offset by the gain in utility to the person undertaxed. But Mill's remark, we believe, was not concerned with the utility of money but with a common sense notion about men's reaction to recognized injustice. In this sense it would be generally agreed that the "evil" of being a victim of injustice is greater than the corresponding "good" of being even an innocent beneficiary of it.

[129] Carver, The Minimum Sacrifice Theory of Taxation, 19 Pol. Sci. Q. 66, 73 (1903).

[130] Or, as it is often put, until the sacrifices at the margin for the two men are equated. Hence, minimum sacrifice is frequently called equi-marginal sacrifice. It is sometimes suggested that such equi-marginal sacrifice is simply a third form of equality of sacrifice. See Dalton, Principles of Public Finance c. IX (15th ed., 1946). This was Edgeworth's device for saving Mill. Edgeworth, II Papers Relating to Political Economy 237 (1925). But equi-marginal sacrifice simply makes no sense as a principle of equalizing sacrifice among individuals.

to the smallest incomes till a dead level of equality is attained. If this latter procedure is ruled out and we are only allowed to impose taxes up to the amount of the
revenue required for the government's needs, this revenue should be collected exclusively from the highest incomes, these being all reduced in the process to the level
of the highest untaxed income.[131]

The proponent of minimum sacrifice does not stop here for long. As
Edgeworth put it, "[t]he *acme* of socialism is thus for a moment sighted;
but it is immediately clouded over by doubts and reservations."[132] The
doubts and reservations of course arise from the unquestionable impact
such 100% marginal tax rates would have on productivity, and the loss of
satisfactions that such lower production would entail. To keep the community sacrifice at a minimum, it is necessary to balance the disadvantage
of lower productivity against the advantage of taxing away only dollars
with the lowest utility.[133] In any practical application, minimum sacrifice
must fall short of the 100% rates it at first appears to dictate. But giving
due recognition to any conceivable assumptions about impairment of incentives, the minimum sacrifice formula, along with a decline in the utility
curve, will dictate some degree of progression.

From one point of view minimum sacrifice would appear to state the
strongest case for progression on sacrifice grounds. One weakness of the
equal sacrifice criterion, and to some extent even the proportionate sacrifice criterion, is that not all declining utility curves result in progression;
something more about the steepness of the curve must be known. In contrast, minimum sacrifice necessarily gives some progression if the money
utility curve declines at all. It requires no knowledge of the utility curve
other than that it declines and thus reduces by one the number of steps
required to reach progression. It is this economy of minimum sacrifice
theory which particularly caught the fancy of Edgeworth. Only minimum
sacrifice, he urged, "in trumpet tones proclaims that the rate of taxation
ought to be progressive."[134]

[131] Pigou, A Study in Public Finance 57–58 (3d rev. ed., 1951).

[132] II Edgeworth, Papers Relating to Political Economy 104 (1925).

[133] Carver, The Ethical Basis of Distribution and Its Application to Taxation, 6 Annals
94–97 (1895). The disadvantages are those outlined in the text, section 5(c) supra.

[134] II Papers Relating to Political Economy 240 (1925). Edgeworth became quite enthusiastic over this economy of assumptions. In replying to Weston, who had criticized minimum
sacrifice on the ground that it assumed no exact relationship between utility and money,
Edgeworth wryly remarked: "This is the first time that the parsimony of assumptions has
been made a reproach to a mathematical argument. After Clerk Maxwell had shown that the
observed laws of pressure and so forth were accounted for by the hypothesis that a gas con-
sisted of an indefinite number of perfectly elastic minute spheres encountering each other in a
molecular chaos . . . was it any imperfection to show that much the same conclusion was deducible even without assuming the sphericity of the molecules?" Ibid., at 239.

While it may be true that if the utility of money declines, minimum sacrifice does give certain progression, it is no better guide than proportionate sacrifice in giving certainty as to the rates. The rate pattern dictated under the proportionate sacrifice formula depends directly on the steepness of the curve. On first approximation minimum sacrifice seems to be free of this source of uncertainty; whatever the slope of the curve the theory would proceed by bringing top level incomes down to the next level and so on until the requisite revenue has been raised. But this certainty is illusory. As noted above, the actual tax rates will depend on estimates of the impact of the rates on incentives, and accordingly an almost complete unknown is introduced into the equation.

And there is a further source of uncertainty as to rates. The conclusion that minimum sacrifice, impairment of productivity aside, would require cutting off the peaks in sequence until the necessary revenue had been raised conceals a questionable assumption. The assumption is that the utility of the last dollar taken in taxes is independent of the total dollars the taxpayer had before taxes. It may be true that to take $2 from a man with $5,002 and to take none from a man with $5,000 entails less total sacrifice than taking $1 from each; but surely it is highly debatable that this is true if in the example the richer man had an income of $10,000, had grown accustomed to this standard of living, and for the first time $4,998 in taxes had just been taken from him. The utility curve purports to describe primarily the value of marginal or last dollars to men with different amounts of money. It states the value of the 5,000th dollar to a man with $5,000 and the value of the 10,000th dollar to a man with $10,000. But it does not state the value of the 5,000th dollar to the man accustomed to $10,000.[135] It would seem not a little arbitrary for sacrifice theory to ignore this additional variable of differential human conditioning, and if it does

[135] "This objection, however, could only apply at the time when the tax was first imposed. At such a time it would doubtless be true that the five thousandth dollar taken from a man with an income of ten thousand would occasion him a greater sacrifice than the taking of the first dollar from an income of five thousand dollars would occasion its owner. But the reasons for this are twofold. In the first place, by taxing the first man so heavily the state would be depriving him of so many things which he was accustomed to enjoying that by the time the five thousandth dollar was reached, the taking of each particular dollar would be keenly felt. The last dollar of his remaining income would represent a greater utility to him than would the last dollar of the five thousand dollar income to its owner. In the second place, by taxing the second man so lightly as compared with his present taxes, the state would be allowing him to consume some things to which he had not become accustomed. The taking of the particular dollar in question would not involve a very high sacrifice, for the reason that it would deprive him only of some enjoyment which had not yet entered into his standard of living. But both these reasons would disappear after the new tax had been in operation for a generation, or long enough to bring the standards of living of the two men to the same level." Carver, The Minimum Sacrifice Theory of Taxation, 19 Pol. Sci. Q. 66, 74–75 (1903). Pigou takes the same position in A Study in Public Finance 90 (3d rev. ed., 1951).

recognize it, it places "the minimum-sacrifice legislator under the unfortunate disability of not knowing where to start."[136]

It is now time to back up and examine the initial assumption of the minimum sacrifice theory—that it is the proper function of the state to legislate in all areas, and particularly in matters of taxation, so as to keep the sacrifice imposed on the community as a whole to a minimum. To some minds, such as Henry Simons,[137] this assumption was the outstanding absurdity of the theory, while to others, such as Edgeworth and Pigou,[138] this adaptation of the utilitarian principle was the single strongest aspect of the minimum sacrifice theory. As a general principle for political decision the minimum sacrifice principle certainly contains some insight into the problem of resolving conflicting individual and group interests. Broadly viewed, it is simply a variant formulation of the quest for the common good or the common welfare. But insofar as the principle has suggested some degree of scientific precision in handling such issues, it has been subjected to serious criticism and is hardly fashionable today. The crux of the criticism has been that it reduces ethics and political science to accounting and that it does not discriminate sufficiently as to the quality of desires or satisfactions.

It may be that taxation lends itself more readily to the kind of quantification the utilitarian principle seems to require, but here the principle must compete at least with equality of sacrifice, particularly proportionate sacrifice. In order to choose between the two principles a further consideration must be noted. If we are not seeking through taxation directly to alter the existing distribution of income but simply to allocate a necessary burden, the principle of minimum sacrifice has little appeal. So long as the discussion is confined to how best to share a burden, the principle seems not a little absurd. At least where two men are both above the subsistence level, it is strange indeed to have them share a common burden

---

[136] Simons, Personal Income Taxation 8 (1938). There does not seem to be a comparable difficulty under the proportionate sacrifice standard since the objective is to come as close as possible to reducing each man's standard of living in the same proportion.

[137] In an elaborate parable Simons posits a world in which individuals are of two classes in terms of their capacity for pleasure. He then asks whether anyone would follow the utilitarian principle and favor taking less away from those who are already blessed with a greater capacity for pleasure. Simons, Personal Income Taxation 12–14 (1938).

[138] II Edgeworth, Papers Relating to Political Economy 117, 131 (1925). Pigou has an interesting discussion of the priority of minimum sacrifice over equal sacrifice as a principle of tax justice. "So far as political theory is concerned, maximum aggregate welfare is everywhere accepted as the right goal of government. . . . In the special field of taxation this general principle is identical with the principle of least sacrifice. Its validity appears to me to be given directly in intuition." Pigou, A Study in Public Finance 43 et seq. (3d rev. ed., 1951).

by putting all of it on the wealthier man. Moreover, if it is assumed for the moment that the utility of money is constant, any method whatsoever of allocating the tax burden would be equally congenial to the minimum sacrifice principle.

But this is, of course, unfair to the doctrine. Minimum sacrifice necessarily challenges the existing distribution of satisfactions, and hence of income or wealth, and in this challenge lies the source of its greatest appeal. In defense of the minimum sacrifice principle Pigou asserts that

people's economic well-being depends on the whole system of law, including the laws of property, contract and bequest, and not merely upon the law about taxes. To hold that the law about taxes ought to affect different people's satisfactions equally, while allowing that the rest of the legal system may properly affect them very unequally, seems not a little arbitrary.[139]

The appeal of minimum sacrifice in these terms is that it commands the state through its laws, including its tax law, to control the distribution of wealth and income so as to maximize satisfactions.[140]

On this interpretation the case for progression on minimum sacrifice grounds merges with the case for progression on the explicit ground of mitigating existing inequalities of wealth or income. The reduction of economic inequality has been one of the principal justifications for progression and will be discussed in detail later. It is sufficient for present purposes to raise a question whether the minimum sacrifice notion has any persuasiveness independently of the frank case for greater economic equality or whether it is merely a circumlocution for a more obvious position.[141] It may be useful to remember that minimum sacrifice commands greater economic equality only so long as it is assumed that the utility of money declines. Would any one who favors progressive taxation on minimum sacrifice grounds not continue to do so on equalitarian grounds if he came to believe that the utility of money was constant?[142]

[139] Pigou, A Study in Public Finance 44 (3d rev. ed., 1951).

[140] It is somewhat ironic that minimum sacrifice should begin as an explicit theory of economic equality and then somewhat lose this directness as it becomes a mathematical tax theory concerned with equi-marginal sacrifice. See note 125 supra. One possible explanation for this divorce is that once minimum sacrifice was conceived to be a tax formula, the revenue goal to which it was to be applied was taken as determined apart from equalitarian considerations. Thus the formula lost its explicit concern with lessening economic inequalities.

[141] "If there is any cogency in these remarks, one may conclude that the case for equality (for less inequality) is enormously stronger than any utility foundation on which it can be rested. . . ." Simons, Personal Income Taxation 14 (1938).

[142] A similar line of argument is used by Chapman in an effort to cast doubt on the validity of the proportionate sacrifice formula. Chapman's formulation also raises the interesting question of whether it is appropriate to prove a reductio ad absurdum by assuming a miracle. Chapman, The Utility of Income and Progressive Taxation, 23 Econ. J. 25, 34 (1913).

12

The analysis of sacrifice doctrine has proceeded by accepting uncritically the basic assumptions underlying it in order to examine how convincing a case for progression can then be made out. Perhaps enough has already been said to indicate that at best the case is not very persuasive. But however modest that case is, it tends to dissolve altogether when the basic assumptions themselves are scrutinized.

The pivotal assumptions can now be restated: (1) units of money can be meaningfully translated into units of utility or satisfaction; (2) in general the relation between utility and money for an individual man is such that a curve for the utility of his money will have a declining slope; (3) and, finally, such a curve will be approximately the same for all men.

However hesitant the proponents of sacrifice theory have been about the slope of the utility curve, by and large they have had no doubts that the curve does decline.[143] If two men are compared, one having an income of $1,000 and the other an income of $100,000, it does not seem very difficult to conclude that the utility of the last dollar to the wealthier man is less than the utility of the last dollar to the other.[144] And this, it is to be noted, is all that is required to hold that money has some declining utility. The conclusion in this example seems intuitively correct. If through introspection we imagine ourselves in the two positions we are likely to feel that the loss of a dollar at the $1,000 level would be quite a different matter than its loss at the $100,000 level.

This conclusion seems corroborated by several other considerations. First it seems to follow from the assumption that a man tries to dispose of his income in a way that maximizes the satisfactions which he can get from it. That is, he arranges to satisfy his most important needs first, and so on down the line. As Lerner puts it:

From this it follows that if income were greater the additional things that would be bought with the increment of income would be things that are rejected when income is smaller because they give less satisfaction; and if income were greater still, even less satisfactory things would be bought.[145]

---

[143] Confidence on this point has even extended to the field of tort liability. See James, Accident Liability Reconsidered: The Impact of Liability Insurance, 57 Yale L.J. 549, 550 n. 1(c) (1948), in which the author finds support for a "wide and regular distribution of losses" by recourse to the declining utility of money. Cf. a note in Marshall, Principles of Economics 135 (8th ed., 1925), making the same point about insurance and also suggesting that the declining utility of money may be invoked as an argument against gambling.

[144] This is not a new insight. Plehn quotes the Indian sage Manu as having made the point somewhere between 1200 and 1500 B.C. Plehn, Introduction to Public Finance 4 (5th ed., 1926).

[145] Lerner, The Economics of Control 26 (1944).

And, conversely, if the income were smaller the last items bought with the lesser income would give greater satisfaction than the items bought with the corresponding last dollars of the present larger income.

Additional confirmation appears to be offered by the impression that if expenditures were examined empirically it would be found that persons on the average tend to have the same general sequence of expenditures as their total incomes increase. That is, the average man buys milk before caviar.

Finally there is the observation that at a very low level of income men seem to be willing to exert great effort to earn an added dollar while at high levels of income they appear to be less willing to increase their effort to earn an added dollar. It thus seems that as men have larger amounts of income they value additional amounts of money less.[146]

But despite its initial plausibility, there are formidable objections to the conclusion. To begin with, it is necessary in comparing the value of money to two men with different incomes to make explicit whether one of them is below the minimum subsistence level or whether both of them are above it. To make a case for progression over and above that which accompanies the exemption of subsistence income it must be shown that the value of money declines for incomes above the exemption level. It is not enough to argue that taking a dollar from a man with less than subsistence income entails more sacrifice than taking a dollar from a man with a very large income.

In further analyzing the question whether money has a declining utility it is also important to put to one side all analogies to the observation that particular commodities have a declining utility to their users.[147] There is no need here to enter into the debate whether it is useful or necessary, in

---

[146] It might seem that additional light on how men value money can be gained by observing their practices in giving to charity. If it is found that the giving is proportionate with income, this might be some evidence against the notion that money is thought to have a declining utility. A finding that giving is progressive with income would be ambiguous. Voluntary giving is itself a form of consumption.

A very rough and informal check into the matter indicated that among persons experienced in raising money for charities, defined broadly, there was no agreement on the criterion for measuring generosity. On the whole it was agreed that giving today is at best proportionate with income, and probably not even that. There is, however, the ambiguity that a scale of gifts proportionate with income before taxes would be progressive with income after taxes.

[147] See Kendrick, The Ability-to-Pay Theory of Taxation, 29 Amer. Econ. Rev. 92 (1939); Adams, The Science of Finance 348 (1898). The fact that money can be saved as well as spent should eliminate the possibility of limiting the utility of money to the range of current consumption. Unlike current consumption there is an indefiniteness about savings. Savings may be viewed as indeterminate future consumption, and this in itself casts doubt on whether the utility of dollars which are saved can be said to decline.

economic theory, to assume that commodities have a declining utility. Money is infinitely versatile. And even if all the things money can buy are subject to a law of diminishing utility, it does not follow that money itself is.

The attempt to buttress the conviction about the declining utility of money by reference to effort at varying income levels also leads nowhere in the end. It would be generally agreed that the more direct way of testing the utility of money is to assume that the acquisition of it was effortless and to look only to the satisfactions which come from having it. Nevertheless, in the absence of more direct means of getting at the question, observations about effort may be circumstantial evidence as to the nature of the money utility curve. The argument that the curve declines asserts that men are less willing to work for an additional dollar the more money they have; it seeks to explain this on the grounds that they must therefore value additional dollars less the more money they have. But this explanation presents several difficulties. First, the facts are hard to come by. If willingness to work more is being measured solely by the time devoted to work, it does not seem to check with common observation to contend that the lower income groups work more hours per day. For one reason or another men in our society at all levels of the income scale seem to work roughly the same amount. If willingness to work more is being measured not by time alone but by the intensity of effort during a given time, there is simply no basis for making comparisons. If conjecture is in order, it would seem that those with higher incomes and more responsible jobs work more intensively as their responsibilities and incomes increase. Second, the argument must assume that the leisure preferences of all men are approximately alike; that is, it assumes that independently of money they value additional leisure the same way. If this were not so, leisure could not furnish a way of "pricing" money. But this is surely a case of the blind leading the blind, since we know even less about the leisure curve than we do about the money utility curve. And if one had to guess, the better guess would seem to be that men's taste for leisure varies more than their taste for money since leisure, somewhat like a particular commodity, is less versatile than money. Third, the data are complicated by the possibility that for some men work has become a form of recreation, a way of spending leisure; and, it might be added, for some men spending leisure is more onerous than working. Finally, the value of leisure must frequently be affected by the amount of money one has and hence by the capacity to realize various forms of leisure, such as travel. The disinclination to work as income increased might then indicate not that a man valued money less but that he valued his now realizable leisure more.[148]

Despite the force of the above considerations it nevertheless would still seem likely that all men do use their incomes so as to maximize their satisfactions. And this seems to hold even after it is recognized that money has infinite versatility. If men do allocate their incomes so as to satisfy their most important wants first, must it be concluded that each addition to their income satisfies a less important want and therefore must have a decreased value to them?

The proposition that men use an increase in income to satisfy a want which they were previously unwilling to satisfy is stated too baldly. The usual statement implies that when a man's income is increased he continues to spend his original income as before and simply adds new items of expenditure as a result of the addition to income. It implies therefore that each man goes through life with a hierarchy of wants which are ranked independently of his income and that as his income increases he simply progressively satisfies these wants, thus always moving to satisfy less important ones. But this view oversimplifies the facts. Although it is agreed that at any income level a man disposes of his income so as to maximize his satisfactions, the process of doing so is not so crudely cumulative. The man who at a relatively low income buys and enjoys a second-hand car usually does not, when his income increases, merely add a new car to his possessions and also continue to hold and enjoy the second-hand car as before.[149] He reviews de novo his total wants in the light of his new

[148] Chapman, The Utility of Income and Progressive Taxation, 23 Econ J. 25, 31 (1913). His essay is an interesting criticism of the meaningfulness of a utility curve for money, although he ultimately favors progression on other grounds. See text, section 13 infra.

It has been suggested that all men ought to be taxed so that they in effect work the same total number of hours for the state. At least as far as earned income is concerned this suggestion would result in a proportionate tax. One popular complaint, at least among the rich, about high progressive rates is that the bulk of their working time is spent working for the state.

Those interested in collecting all the theories ever advanced in behalf of progression might note: Godard, Graduated Taxation, 5 Econ. Rev. 39 (1895), where the author argued that the true standard of equality of sacrifice is "sacrifice of energy involving equal tension in its expenditure." Ibid., at 44. Cf. Walker, The Bases of Taxation, 3 Pol. Sci. Q. 1 (1888), where the author argued that a tax on income penalized those who had made the best use of their abilities while relieving the indolent. He proposed, therefore, the native or acquired capacity to earn income rather than the actual income earned as the proper base for taxation.

[149] "The mere fact that, when I have £200 a year, I buy six imitation Chippendale chairs, rather than a single genuine one which costs as much as the other six put together, proves that I prefer the six imitations to the one original chair when I have an income of £200 a year. But it does not prove that, when I have the larger income and have bought the costly chair, and compare my enjoyment of it under the new income conditions with my enjoyment of the six cheap chairs under the old income conditions—that then I must judge the former enjoyment to have been greater than the latter." Chapman, The Utility of Income and Progressive

total income. The process of maximizing his satisfactions from a given amount of income is the process of selecting uses of income so as to strike a balance or harmony among them. It is not plausible that the most important wants of a man with a $5,000 income remain his most important wants when he has an income of $25,000. As his income changes his way of life changes. He becomes in effect a man with a different hierarchy of wants and values. In the end, all that can be told from the data is that when a man has $5,000 he prefers most the uses he then makes of his income and that when he has $25,000 he again prefers most the uses he makes of his income.[150]

If there is any doubt left about the futility of attempting to derive a utility curve from the premise that men always try to maximize their satisfactions from any given amount of money, that doubt surely disappears when the next step is considered. To fit the demands of sacrifice theory the utility curve must be a curve not for a particular man but for men in general. By an examination of the sequence in which each man satisfies his wants it is not possible to make the necessary interpersonal comparisons. In a forceful passage Lionel Robbins underscores this objection. After noting that the order of an individual's preferences has made it possible to construct a theory of exchange, which explains relative prices, he continues:

But it is one thing to assume that scales can be drawn up showing the *order* in which an individual will prefer a series of alternatives, and to compare the arrangement of one such individual scale with another. It is quite a different thing to assume that behind such arrangements lie magnitudes which themselves can be compared. . . . Suppose that a difference of opinion were to arise about A's preferences. Suppose that I thought that, at certain prices, he preferred *n* to *m*, and you thought that, at the same prices, he preferred *m* to *n*. It would be easy to settle our differences in a purely scientific manner. Either we could ask A to tell us. Or, if we refused to believe that introspection on A's part was possible, we could expose him to the stimuli in question and observe his behavior. . . . But suppose that we differed about the satisfaction derived by A from an income of £1,000 and the satisfaction derived by B from an income of twice that magnitude. Asking them would provide no solution. Supposing they differed. A might urge that he had more satisfaction than B at the margin. While B might urge that, on the contrary, he had more satisfaction than A. We do not need to be slavish behaviorists to realize that here is no scientific evidence. *There is no means of testing the magnitude of A's satisfaction as compared with B's.* . . .[151]

Taxation, 23 Econ. J. 25, 32 (1913). See also Cohen-Stuart, A Contribution to the Theory of the Progressive Income Tax (1889) (Ms. trans., Te Velde, University of Chicago Libraries, 1936) 96–98.

[150] This would be equally true as his income declines.

[151] Robbins, Nature and Significance of Economic Science 138–40 (2d ed., 1935). Stamp puts the point less formally: "[I]t is very difficult for a man to say quantitatively that one boot

Thus the only remaining way to establish that money has a declining utility is sheer intuition. We may still be confident, despite the above analysis, that if we had many times the amount of money we now have we would place a lesser value on an additional dollar. The majority of men would probably confess to a similar intuition about themselves.[152] But here again the step needed to complete the argument stumbles on the problem of interpersonal comparisons. The argument can only proceed on the assumption that the money utility curve for yourself, which you derive from introspection, also holds true for other men in the society. This further hypothesis, which can only be "tested" by intuition, has been found to be utterly arbitrary by some. To quote again from Lionel Robbins, "Introspection does not enable A to measure what is going on in B's mind, nor B to measure what is going on in A's. There is no way of comparing the satisfactions of different people."[153] But others have found the assumption that all men react in the same way to varying amounts of money to be congenial. Pigou observes:

In the ordinary affairs of life, while recognizing the existence of individual idiosyncrasies, racial differences, differences due to habit and training and so on, we always assume that groups of *prima facie* similar men will be mentally affected by similar situations in much the same way; that they will get roughly equal enjoyment from a dish of ham and eggs and will suffer a roughly similar sacrifice from surrendering their seat in a railway carriage. We *expect* similar situations to produce similar mental effects, and it is only when they seem not to do so that in normal non-philosophic moods that we think there is something to explain.[154]

------

pinches *three* times as much as the other, even where both are his own, and how much more difficult is it for one man to say that his boot pinches *twice* as much as another's!" Stamp, Fundamental Principles of Taxation 53–54 (1921).

[152] This probably explains why so many persons have thought that progression was "instinctively correct." One trouble with acting upon such an intuition is that it is likely to lead to a kind of psychological irresponsibility which parallels the political irresponsibility sometimes charged to progression. It would not be too surprising to find that the sureness with which the declining utility of money is intuitive varies inversely with one's income.

[153] Robbins, Nature and Significance of Economic Science 139–40 (2d ed., 1935). The objection has been a long standing one. Daniels, Elements of Public Finance 87–88 (1899); Chapman, The Utility of Income and Progressive Taxation, 23 Econ. J. 25, 33 (1913).

[154] Pigou, A Study in Public Finance 41–42 (3d rev. ed., 1951). Carver takes the same stand: "Such an application of the principle involves the assumption that wants are equal, which, though obviously not true, approximates more nearly to the truth than any other working assumption that could possibly be invented. Since the state must collect a revenue, it must have some definite assumption upon which it can proceed. The question is not, therefore, whether men's wants are equal, but whether there is any rule of inequality of wants upon which the apportionment of taxes could be made with a nearer approximation to the truth. If there be such a rule, it has not yet been discovered. To assume, for example, that the man whose income is greater than five thousand has correspondingly greater wants than the man whose income is less than five thousand, would be obviously unsafe, because there are even chances that the opposite would be true. Where the chances are even on both sides, it is safer to assume equality. Of a given number of men of the same age and the same general standard of health

If there is no way of deriving a money utility curve other than by intro-spection it would seem pretty clear that neither those who concur with Robbins nor those who agree with Pigou can be moved from their position on this issue.[155]

Of course if one holds the Robbins' position about interpersonal com-parisons, one is not merely rejecting the notion that money has declining utility for all men. Rather one is rejecting once and for all the possibility of using sacrifice analysis as a guide to tax policy. If, however, one sees the commonality of men as Pigou sees it, it may be well to take a last look at the insight which a man gets when he tries to discover by introspection his own utility curve for money. He is likely to find he is entering the realm of paradox.

Let him assume that he is reasonably happy at present and then let him reflect on how he would feel if his income were to increase enormously. If money always has some value then the aggregate increase in the satis-factions he anticipates will be very great. But as he reflects more deeply he is likely to conclude that such an increase in his income could not produce any comparable increase in his total happiness. He might get some cor-roboration for this by observing that the very rich are not as much happier than the rest as utility theory would appear to dictate. If they are not, this might be explained by assuming that money has a dizzily steep declining utility, and that it has virtually no utility after a moderate amount has been obtained. Or it might be explained by assuming that money is a trivial component in the whole that makes for happiness. But the first assumption is hard to square with the fact that men continue to

(by way of illustration) it is obviously untrue to assume that they will all live the same number of years, yet it is nearer the truth to assume that than any other definite workable principle. Consequently the life-insurance company acts justly when it assumes that they will live the same number of years, and apportions their premiums accordingly." Carver, The Minimum Sacrifice Theory of Taxation, 19 Pol. Sci. Q. 66, 74–75 (1903).

[155] In many areas the law ignores individual differences and acts on the assumption that men are the same. Perhaps the most interesting of these for present purposes arises in connection with setting the standard of care for negligence. While there is some uncertainty as to how much subjective factors are considered, it is unanimously agreed that to some extent the indi-vidual's exact capacities will be ignored when he fails to act like a reasonable man. The law's abstracting of individual differences is on firmer grounds here than in theorizing about the utility of money. First, there is more accessible evidence of the common capacities of the ma-jority of men, such as to drive a car in a certain way. Second, unless an absolute liability ap-proach is to be adopted, the law must set a standard most men can satisfy and cannot stop for an elaborate inquiry into individual capacities in each case. Finally, the law is concerned with setting a rule which will affect the conduct of other men, and the theory is that more harm will result by relaxing the standard than by compelling men to act at the peril of not acting like reasonable men. The classic statement of the theory is Holmes, The Common Law c. 3 (1881). See also Seavey, Negligence—Subjective or Objective, 41 Harv. L. Rev. 1 (1927); cf. James and Dickinson, Accident Proneness and Accident Law, 63 Harv. L. Rev. 769 (1950).

desire more money and that they are willing to work for it. And the second assumption relegates money to such an insignificant position that the whole question of justice in taxation is deprived of its significance.

The paradox is an ancient one. Men have long speculated over whether the man in the palace is happier than the man in the cottage.[156] On the one hand there is no doubt that money is a good and that it is desirable. On the other hand it seems that whenever we try to state more precisely its relationship to happiness the result approaches an absurdity. The error lies in trying to translate money, which can be measured in definite units, into corresponding units of satisfaction or well-being. In the end satisfaction in the sense of happiness defies quantification.[157] Utility is a meaningful concept; units of utility are not. It is in the face of this difficulty that, even waiving all other objections, the whole elaborate analysis of progression in terms of sacrifice and utility doctrine finally collapses.[158]

[156] "I think, however, that the sentimental optimism which held that happiness is equally distributed between the palace and the cottage—with a preference, if at all, in favour of the cottage—has wellnigh vanished before a more careful and impartial study of the facts of social existence. At the present day, even those who most warmly assail Political Economy on the ground of the exaggerated importance which it attaches to wealth, do not usually go so far as to maintain that increase of wealth is not important for the individual and for society so far as it can be obtained without any sacrifice of other sources of happiness. It is, indeed, probable that there are many rich individuals who would be happier on the whole if they were poorer; and, again, that the immediate effect of a sudden and considerable increase in the wealth of certain sections of the poorer classes might very likely be a diminution of happiness, on account of the increase of pernicious indulgences that it would bring with it. But, making all allowance for such partial or transitory exceptions, it remains true that the practical reasonings of the great mass of mankind—whether for themselves or for others in whom they are individually interested—proceed on the assumption that it is an advantage to be richer; and, further, that the judgment of the most highly cultivated, scrupulously moral and sincerely religious persons—as expressed in their conduct—does not diverge materially from that of the vulgar in the matter. The *elite* certainly disagree very much with the vulgar as to the real value of particular purchaseable commodities; but they do not practically doubt that additional control over purchaseable commodities generally is an important gain to an individual who obtains it. A man who chose poverty for himself, except for some manifest special and unpurchaseable advantage, or at the manifest call of some special duty, would be deemed eccentric: a man who chose it for his wife and children would be generally thought to deserve a harsher name." Sidgwick, The Principles of Political Economy 519–20 (2d ed., 1887).

[157] But note Pigou: "We all know that we are happier—enjoying more satisfaction—at one time than at another and that some events inflict on us greater sacrifices than others. Whether we can properly claim to feel, say, 'twice' as happy or suffer 'twice' as large a sacrifice of satisfaction on some occasions as on others is more doubtful; but that is not required. Different satisfactions and sacrifices to the same person *are* quantitatively comparable." Pigou, A Study in Public Finance 41 (3d rev. ed., 1951).

[158] It is somewhat amusing to attempt to interpret our present personal income tax rates on the hypothesis that they were set in accordance with sacrifice theory. A brief attempt to do this is found in Preinreich, The Theory of Progressive Taxation, 25 Taxes 742 (1947).

As farewell questions about utility curves it might be asked: What do changes in the rate pattern of a tax imply about the curve, at least under the equal sacrifice and proportionate sacrifice formulas? And what does the split income arrangement, introduced by the Revenue Act of 1948, imply about the curve for married persons as contrasted with single individuals?

13

While sacrifice analysis is less fashionable today than it was a generation ago, there is still a popular idea that taxes should be levied in accordance with the respective abilities of the taxpayers to pay. In fact it is not
infrequently urged that ability to pay is the cardinal criterion of tax justice. Stated this briefly, ability to pay does furnish a slogan with emotive
appeal to which almost everyone can subscribe. The difficulty, of course,
is that the key phrase is so ambiguous that the slogan lacks any content.
But since some attempts employing the terminology of ability to pay have
been made to establish a case for progression, it is in order to consider
briefly whether in any of its versions ability to pay adds to the prior
analysis.

There is at least one traditional usage of ability to pay which is helpful,
although not in connection with progression. If the issue is that of selecting an appropriate tax base, it is meaningful to state a preference for one
base as against another on the grounds of ability to pay.[159] Much of the
long fight over establishing income as the tax base was couched in these
terms; income, it was urged, is the best test of the ability of the taxpayer
to pay taxes. This is simply a way of saying that a tax on income is better
than a tax on any less inclusive base, such as property or particular items
of consumption, inasmuch as it is a better index of the dollars accessible
for taxes.

Such a limited meaning for ability, once the base has been decided upon,
tells nothing about the relative capacities of taxpayers. To get progression
under an income tax out of notions of ability to pay requires the thesis
that ability increases more rapidly than income. Many of the supporters
of this thesis turn out, upon scrutiny, to have been talking obliquely about
sacrifice. Tax ability is the ability to bear a burden, that is, to tolerate a
sacrifice. Obviously this line of analysis permits the conclusion that a taxpayer with twice the income of another, above the minimum subsistence
level, has at least twice the ability to bear the burden of taxes. But to
argue that he has more than twice the ability, as progression would require, is to argue that he feels the sacrifice less per dollar. Ability then is
but a less lucid way of approaching money as having declining utility. In
this sense ability to pay is the inverse of sacrifice or utility.

Some writers, conscious of this confusion, have explicitly given ability
to pay a meaning which is at least in part independent of sacrifice. One
endeavor has been to shift from the sacrifice involved in giving up income

[159] Buehler, Ability to Pay, 1 Tax Law Rev. 243 (1946).

to the "faculty" or ease of earning it. The leading analysis of this type was that offered by Professor Seligman who, after distinguishing between acquisition and consumption of income, went on to say:

it is evident that the possession of large fortunes or large incomes in itself affords the possessor a decided advantage in augmenting his possessions. The facility of increasing production frequently grows in more than arithmetical proportion. A rich man may be said to be subject to a certain sense to a law of increasing returns. The more he has, the easier it is for him to acquire still more. . . . While the native power of production . . . remains as before, this "acquired power" has greatly augmented. Hence from the point of view of production faculty may be said to increase more rapidly than fortune or income. This element of taxable capacity would hence not illogically result in a more than proportionate rate of taxation.[160]

It is especially noteworthy that Seligman found in this the only satisfactory justification for progression, and that he came to it only after an exhaustive study of the literature.[161]

There are one or two difficulties with this faculty approach. It does not purport to cover by far the largest class of income, that from rendering services. Nor would any extension of it to such "earned" income be feasible. It is true that it is easier for a man who is paid $10 per hour to earn a dollar than it is for the man who is paid $1 per hour. But this relationship is fully reflected in a proportionate tax. Thus the faculty approach at best would not support a general income tax that was progressive. There may be some sense in distinguishing between the cost of acquiring all "earned" income on the one hand and all income from investments or capital on the other, and this distinction frequently has been strongly urged as a reason for taxing these two classes of income at different rates.[162] Whatever the

[160] Seligman, Progressive Taxation in Theory and Practice 291–92 (2d rev. ed., 1908). The Seligman version of faculty was composed not only of the ease of acquiring money, but also retained the orthodox notion of the sacrifice of parting with money in taxes. This is especially noteworthy because Seligman explicitly rejected orthodox sacrifice theory, standing alone, as being too uncertain and unscientific. The Seligman combination moved Edgeworth to remark: "It was a master-stroke of practical wisdom to include the distributional, as well as the productional, criterion of taxation under the category of 'faculty,' which has the appearance of being more definite than the *summum genus* utility. . . . To one who believes in the double nature of the fiscal summum bonum the happy ambiguity of the proposed canon renders it all the more acceptable. It has a Parliamentary sound. It is like the celebrated resolution of the House of Commons declaring the throne vacant after the flight of James II; in which, Macaulay says, 'There was a phrase for every subdivision of the majority. The one beauty of the resolution was its inconsistency.'" II Edgeworth, Papers Relating to Political Economy 241–42 (1925).

[161] In fairness to Seligman it should be noted that he never found that there was more than a very modest balance of considerations favoring progression. This may also have some relevance for his influence in keeping progression respectable. See note 176 infra.

[162] Differentiation between "earned" and "unearned" income has long been a major item of controversy in the income tax, especially in England. For many years in England the issue of differentiation was much more prominent than the issue of progression. See generally U.S. Treas. Dep't Study, The Tax Treatment of Earned Income (1947).

merits of such differentiation, it does not result in progression unless one makes the odd assumption that the "unearned" income portion of total income becomes an increasingly larger component of total income as total income increases.[163] In any event if differentiation is the objective there would be no excuse for not attempting to separate directly the two classes of income.

It remains to ask whether the Seligman theory does justify applying progressive rates to "unearned" incomes of varying amounts. Consider first the case in which two investors have the same amount of capital but secure different rates of return. Presumably there would be no justification here for taxing the larger return at a higher rate of tax. The larger return reflects either compensation for assuming a greater risk or a reward for superior judgment or the result of luck. Next consider two investors with different amounts of capital who secure the same rate of return. The equivalence of the rate of return would seem to be sufficient evidence that, all other things being equal, the earning faculty of capital does not increase as capital increases. Finally consider the case in which two investors have different amounts of capital and in which the wealthier secures a higher rate of return. This must be the case from which Seligman was generalizing and, if so, it would seem a gross error to treat this as the typical case. But, confining attention to this limited case, it does not afford any more justification for taxing the higher return at a higher rate of tax than did the first case. Once again the difference in rates of return is readily explainable in terms of a differential in risk, judgment, or luck. Even if there is another explanation, and it is difficult to think of one, it surely would be exceedingly arbitrary to rely solely on it in allocating the tax burden.[164]

Another way of giving content to ability to pay was suggested by the

[163] There are many variations on this formula as a means of justifying progression. The general formula is: x is the component of income which is taken to be the correct base for the tax; x cannot be isolated conveniently; but it is believed to increase more rapidly than income. Therefore a progressive tax on income is a good approximation of the ideally correct tax.

[164] The view that money makes money in Seligman's sense has been taken seriously. "In terms of our actual world, the possession of wealth or the receipt of income is itself an evidence of faculty or power not only to pay taxes out of one's income but also to earn additional income. Money earns money. The first thousand dollars 'comes the hardest.' He who has a bank account has three hands: his right hand, his left hand, and his bank account." Groves, Financing Government 39 (rev. ed., 1946). Fagan discusses the Seligman faculty theory sympathetically in Recent and Contemporary Theories of Progressive Taxation, 46 J. Pol. Econ. 457, 485-90 (1938). See also Hunter, Outlines of Public Finance 146 (rev. ed., 1926). A different interpretation of the money-makes-money point might give it greater validity but less relevance for progression. It might be taken to mean that a monopoly position or special access to inside information may accompany large incomes.

British economist J. A. Hobson.[165] Stated simply his case for progression on ability to pay grounds involves three steps. First, income is broken down into two components, that part which is considered a "cost" of production and that part which is not such a cost and therefore is "surplus." Next, it is asserted that only the surplus portion represents ability to pay taxes, and the whole of the surplus can properly be taken in taxes. Finally, since surplus cannot be identified directly, it is located indirectly and this is done by assuming that as income increases surplus increases even more rapidly.

The terms "costs" and "surplus" have special meanings for Hobson:

Those elements of income which are necessary payments to owners of productive agents, in order to sustain the productive efficiency of an agent and to evoke its application, rank as "costs" of production, and have no ability to bear taxation. . . . The elements of income which are not "costs" are "surplus." All economic rents of land . . . all interest, profits, and other payments for the use of capital, brains or labor, which are due to superior economic opportunities and are not necessary incentives to secure such use, will rank as surplus. All forms of surplus have a full ability to bear taxation.[166]

The difficulties with the Hobson theory of progression are legion. Even viewed with the greatest sympathy, his notion of surplus is so fuzzy that such an element would be vastly difficult to identify. When this unknown is coupled with the bald assumption that it increases more rapidly than income, in effect the case for progression is being established by pure fiat. This would be a sufficient basis for dismissing the theory insofar as it relates to progression. But even if the Hobsonian surplus could be located with precision there would be no justification for making it specially eligible for taxation. Take the traditional case of economic rent of land, which can be defined as the amount of rent paid on better land in excess of that paid on the poorest land in use. It is this difference which Hobson regards as surplus and which should be taken for taxes since none of the production of the better land will be lost as a result of the tax, and since such economic rent is in the nature of a windfall. Whatever the position of the original owner of the best land, there is no windfall rent to the subsequent purchaser since the economic rent in a normal market must have been fully reflected in the price he had to pay for the land. And even in the case of the original owner, while there was clear gain, there was no windfall; all investment involves risk-taking and it is unreal to look only to the

---

[165] Hobson, Taxation in the New State (1919). There are discussions of Hobson in Fagan, Recent and Contemporary Theories of Progressive Taxation, 46 J. Pol. Econ. 490–93 (1938), and Stamp, Principles of Taxation 42–43 (1921).

[166] Hobson, Taxation in the New State 41–43 (1919).

successful instances of risk-taking.[167] The rewards to the successful are approximately offset by the losses to the unsuccessful risk-takers. There is thus no justification for singling out economic rent as the subject for taxation, even if it could be identified.

Some brief attention should be reserved for one other attempt to give special meaning to faculty or ability to pay, that of the Vermont economist H. W. Peck.[168] His theory has what must surely be a unique claim to distinction: under it the less rapid the decline in the utility of money the more progressive the tax. In an analysis that strongly reflects the thinking of Seligman and Hobson, Peck sought to establish a kind of "consumer's surplus" as the prime test of taxpaying ability. He defined this surplus as the difference between the cost of acquiring a given amount of income and the utility of it to its possessor. As to the cost, he meant simply the effort involved in acquiring income, and he thought it would be roughly equal for all incomes.[169] Hence he believed that a curve depicting the cost of acquiring a dollar of income would approximate a rectangular hyperbola. As to the utility of money, he thought it declined very slowly and contended that as civilization progressed the utility of additional amounts of money increased because there were more advantageous ways of spending it. The amount of consumer's surplus he defined as the spread between the two curves; and accordingly the less steep the utility curve the greater the spread and therefore the more steep the progression in tax rates.[169] This theory appears to be heir to all the difficulties with the utility and ability theories previously examined, and has as well some of its own.

14

What has been said suggests the tantalizing combination of plausible, ingenious and improbable ideas which make up the case for progression in terms of sacrifice and ability to pay. It likewise suggests why these notions have such a stubborn appeal. But it tends to demonstrate that the hold of these notions on the general public must derive from the fallacies that have frequented the theories and not from their truths which are difficult to drive to and once found would not support any firm conviction about the validity of the progressive principle.

The general appeal of utility and sacrifice doctrine is likely explained

[167] See Daniels, Elements of Public Finance 85 (1899).

[168] Peck, Taxation and Welfare (1925).

[169] A notable feature of Peck's presentation is the drawing of tentative curves for "a savage," "a sensible, intelligent person," and "an industrial titan." Ibid., at 256–57. Another feature is his concept of the "ability to receive" which "in the case of the poor" is the counterpart "to the ability to pay taxes on the part of the rich." Ibid., at 116.

further by another consideration. The ostensibly scientific form of sacrifice theory, which purports to deal with the way people actually react to money, frequently conceals a normative judgment either about the way that people ought to value money[170] or about the social value of typical expenditures at different levels of income. On occasion this latter judgment has been made explicit and a case for progression rested on it. For example, S. J. Chapman argued that:

the wants satisfied by the earlier increments to income are usually of more importance socially than the wants satisfied by later increments to income, whether the satisfaction of the former causes more utility or not. In speaking of the equity of taxation, we are obviously talking ethics, and therefore the wants primarily dealt with must be adjudged not according to the value of their satisfaction in fact (positive value), but according to the value of their satisfaction in a moral scheme of consumption (normative value).[171]

Some of the force of this observation disappears when the area of discussion is confined explicitly to a comparison of persons all of whom have incomes above the minimum subsistence level. Be that as it may, the very ideal of a "moral scheme of consumption" is distasteful. Presumably it is one of the virtues of a free society that, within the widest limits, men are free to maximize their satisfactions according to their own hierarchy of preferences—to prefer baseball games to long essays. This is not to say that education in tastes is not a concern of society; it is only to note that there is great danger in its going beyond education as a means of obtaining such progress. But in any event, in making some of the more obvious conjectures about a "moral" ranking of expenditures, it does not seem promising to try to establish that the average expenditures of the less wealthy are any more worthy than the average expenditures of the more wealthy.[172] This is particularly true if the social importance of savings and investment are taken into account.

Such reflection strongly suggests that the concern is not with the ways in which the more wealthy and the less wealthy actually spend given

[170] Although no one appears to have taken quite this position, an interesting defense for progression might be attempted on the grounds that it reflects the way people *ought to* value money. But perhaps the clearer statement of this view is simply that people ought to favor more equality. It is also suggestive of a possible interpretation of progression as an attempt to coerce through the state a distribution that would be commendable had it resulted from voluntary charity. Compare Carver, The Minimum Sacrifice Theory of Taxation, 19 Pol. Sci. Q. 66 (1904).

[171] Chapman, The Utility of Income and Progressive Taxation, 23 Econ. J. 25, 34 (1913). Compare Beale, The Measure of Income for Taxation, 19 J. Pol. Econ. 655, 661 (1911).

[172] Stamp, while giving this approach some approval as it dealt with lower incomes, thought it lost all validity when applied to the relative social importance of the wants satisfied by the well to do, the rich and the very rich. Stamp, Fundamental Principles of Taxation 45–46 (1921).

amounts of money. Instead the concern is with the desirability of having the less wealthy[173] rather than the more wealthy spend the money. This again leads directly to the case for progression on grounds of mitigating economic inequality, a case which remains to be examined on its own merits.

15

However uncertain other aspects of progression may be, there is one thing about it that is certain. A progressive tax on income necessarily operates to lessen the inequalities in the distribution of that income. In fact, as was noted at the outset, progression cannot be defined meaningfully without reference to its redistributive effect on wealth or income. It would seem therefore that any consideration of progression must at some time confront the issue of equality.

Although there is a very considerable literature on equality, and progressive taxation occupies some role in it, in the literature on progression there has been surprisingly little discussion of the equality issue. A prominent position in the tax literature is that stated with characteristic gusto by Professor Seligman who, it will be recalled, upheld progression on ability to pay grounds:

If the equalizing of fortunes were one of the acknowledged functions of government, it would be useless to perfect any science of finance. There would be only one simple principle: confiscate the property of the rich and give it to the poor. The socialist argument, which undoubtedly lies at the basis for many of the demands for progressive taxation, must be unconditionally rejected by all who are not prepared to classify themselves as socialists. . . . It is quite possible to repudiate absolutely the socialist theory of taxation and yet at the same time advocate progression. One may be an arch individualist and yet logically believe in progressive taxation.[174]

The inappropriateness of explicitly predicating progression on equalitarian grounds has been put a little more diplomatically by Sir Josiah Stamp, who also favored progression on other grounds:

In my judgment, progressive taxation has the happy result of assisting to rectify inequalities, many of which are not economically or ethically justifiable, but it does not *exist* to do this and it has its justification quite apart from this.[175]

This tradition of separating progression from equalitarianism, and softpeddling its redistributive effects, probably served an important function

[173] Or the state; see discussion in the text, section 22 infra.

[174] Seligman, The Theory of Progressive Taxation, 8 Pol. Sci. Q. 220, 222 (1893). Compare Taylor: "If, however, progressive taxation is recognized as the application of a principle (such as ability to pay), it must never be made a principle of itself; for that would be confiscation." Taylor, The Income Tax, 206 Quart. Rev. 331, 335 (1907).

[175] Stamp, Principles of Taxation 177 (1921).

in keeping progression a respectable idea in our society.[176] Yet one can only sympathize with Henry Simons in insisting that, in any discussion of progression, the problem of inequality "be dragged out into the open."[177] Certainly both on grounds of candor and clarity this is commendable. It nevertheless has one overwhelming difficulty. In a study of progression, as soon as the issue of economic inequality has been dragged out into the open, we discover that we have lost our topic.

In substance the issue of progression and equality is simply the great issue of equality itself. If one is persuaded that the society should reduce economic inequalities there are no real problems which specially concern the use of progression to accomplish that result. Despite much rhetoric to the contrary there is no sense to the position that, while other laws might legitimately be used to achieve greater equality, the tax system must not be given over to such a function. The fact is that a progressive income tax may well have some distinctive advantages as a way of redistributing income. There are not so many methods of accomplishing peaceful redistribution. Such measures as government wage and price controls or the exercise of monopoly power by labor unions or industrial combines, although they alter the distribution of economic goods, may well not do so in the direction of a general lessening of inequalities. In any event they all seem to involve a direct interference with the operation of the market or a potentially ominous expansion of government activity and power.[178] By

[176] There are temperate discussions of the question of economic equality and taxation before the turn of the century by such writers as Sidgwick, Adams, and Carver. The Seligman approach makes a sharp division between the equalitarian and other defenses for progression. Thus he is extremely critical of Adolph Wagner who not only favored the use of taxation directly to bring about greater equality, but also contended that all other discussions of progression in terms of ability, sacrifice or benefit had meaning only in this connection. The Seligman approach thus kept progression respectable at the price of consciously ignoring the central issue of equality. A great virtue of Simons was his insistence on bringing the discussion back again to the equality issue.

The development is especially curious in that the minimum sacrifice doctrine, which is predominantly equalitarian, has remained a "respectable" doctrine throughout.

One can only speculate as to what the constitutional career of progression would have been had the case for it at all times been stated frankly on equality grounds; see text, section 3 supra.

[177] Simons, Personal Income Taxation 18 (1938). And see Blough, The Argument Phase of Taxpayer Politics, 17 Univ. Chi. L. Rev. 604, 608 (1950): "The argument that taxation should be used deliberately to alter the distribution of income and wealth is a delicate one to present, at least in these bald terms, and may boomerang. . . . The emotional content of reactions to arguments [of this type] is commonly very high."

[178] See Simons' bitter comparison of progression and unionism. "[P]rogressive taxation is a workable, democratic method for dealing with inequality. The alternative of unionists is to send workers out in packs to exploit and expropriate by devices which resemble those of bandit armies. The one device is inherently orderly, peaceful, gradualist, and efficient. It is the device of law. The other is inherently violent, disruptive, and wasteful in the extreme. One calls for debate, discussion, and political action; the other, for fighting and promiscuous expropriation." Simons, Some Reflections on Syndicalism, 52 J. Pol. Econ. 19 (1944).

using the tax system for redistribution, the market, at least within large limits, can be left to determine relative values and allocate resources through the price mechanism, with the freedom of individuals left relatively unimpaired, with no significant addition to government manpower, and with no increase in difficult discretionary judgments which government personnel need make.

It might be thought that one difficulty with using the tax system as a vehicle of redistribution is that the amount of redistribution would be determined by the amount of revenue and that the revenue total is determined by considerations which need have no connection with redistribution. This difficulty disappears when it is realized that the revenue total itself can be increased in order to transfer income from one group in the society to another. In fact some such transfer payments affect the revenue goal under our present tax structure. If there is any disadvantage in employing taxation as a means of lessening economic inequality it is that the process tends to conceal precisely what is being done about redistribution. It may seem just a nice job of social engineering to have greater equality achieved as a by-product of raising the necessary revenue, for then the society is not simply and nakedly engaged in redistributing income. On the other hand this may be an advantage; it may make politically feasible a goal which otherwise might prove too divisive and put too great a strain on democratic processes.

Having lost our special topic of progression we are now confronted with a dilemma. The larger subject of economic equality either may be not amenable to discussion or it may admit of infinite discussion. One's position about economic inequality may be kept within the confines of a simple statement of preference and nothing more. The approach of Henry Simons is instructive in this regard. A serious student of progressive tax theory, he chose to state his own ultimate case for progression in a single sentence. "The case for drastic progression in taxation must be rested on the case against inequality—on the ethical or aesthetic judgment that the prevailing distribution of wealth and income reveals a degree (and/or kind) of inequality which is distinctly evil or unlovely."[179] This approach to the problem of necessity forecloses any further discussion.

The opposite to so summary an approach is found in the treatment of the equality theme in the socialist literature. Here it is part of a discussion which calls into question the fundamental economic organization of society. Such discussion immediately challenges the institutions of private property, the market and the enterprise system. And this in turn raises

[179] Simons, Personal Income Taxation 18–19 (1938).

other major problems, including the role of the family, the efficiency of central planning, and the long run compatibility of economic planning and political freedoms of the individual. There is of course a definite role for a progressive tax in such a program; and in this context progression has long received support from communist and socialist writers.[180] The case for progression in these terms is at least as strong as the case for socialism. But to examine with appropriate care the issues of socialism would be to go far beyond the tolerable bounds of an essay of this sort.

The interesting thing for our purposes is that the goal of mitigating inequality has not been a socialist monopoly. It has been shared by many who are by no means ready to give up the institutions of private property and private enterprise. It is true that one can without any logical inconsistency defend progression on other than equalitarian grounds even though it necessarily redistributes wealth or income.[181] But today one is not likely to do so with any enthusiasm unless he has made peace with the issue of equality. It may be as Stamp observed in this connection that "We have all heard that it is wrong to marry for money, but quite praiseworthy to marry where money happens to be."[182] This is a fine line to draw

[180] This is as good a place as any to quote the Communist Manifesto. "The proletariat will use its political supremacy to wrest, by degrees, all capital from the bourgeoisie, to centralize all instruments of production in the hands of the state. . . . Of course in the beginning this cannot be effected except by means of despotic inroads on the rights of property and on the conditions of bourgeoisie production. . . . [T]hese measures of course will be different in different countries. Nevertheless in the most advanced countries the following will be pretty generally applicable: . . . 2. A heavy progressive or graduated income tax." Communist Manifesto 152 (1948).

For the socialist approach to taxation and equality see generally Tawney, Equality (1929); Dalton, Some Aspects of the Inequality of Incomes in Modern Communities (1935); Wedgwood, The Economics of Inheritance (1929); Jones, Taxation Yesterday and Tomorrow (1921). "The redistribution of wealth carried through in recent years may well prove to be the most significant, and the most lasting, of all the economic consequences of the policies of the Labor Party. The chief weapon employed for that purpose has been a steeply progressive income tax." Jewkes, Socialism's Legacy to Churchill, Fortune 79, 80 (Dec. 1951).

The rhetorical possibilities of guilt by association here have not been overlooked by the opponents of progression. Compare Lutz who, while admitting that one might well advocate progression without being a communist or even a socialist, goes on to say that such advocates nevertheless become the unwitting collaborators of those who seek the "destruction of the private enterprise system." Lutz, Guideposts to a Free Economy 73 (1945). See also Crotty, A Few Observations: The Communist Manifesto in America, 37 A.B.A.J. 413, 414 (1951): "The second idea which was absorbed by the democracies from the Communist Manifesto with the greatest fervor is the imposition of a heavy progressive or graduated income tax."

[181] The clearest example of this is the advocacy of proportionate sacrifice on the assumption that the utility of money declines; in effect this approach seeks to redistribute money in order not to redistribute satisfactions. See text, section 9 supra. Cohen-Stuart has an extended discussion of the compatibility of proportionate sacrifice and the acceptance of the existing distribution of income. Cohen-Stuart, A Contribution to the Theory of the Progressive Income Tax (1889) (Ms. trans., Te Velde, University of Chicago Libraries, 1936) c. V.

[182] Stamp, Principles of Taxation 170 (1921).

in matters of the heart and perhaps too fine a line to be drawn any longer in matters of taxation. What remains to be examined then is the possible rationale for desiring to lessen economic inequalities within the confines of a private enterprise and market system.

16

It may be useful to begin by speculating about our reactions to the issue of equality if by a convenient miracle the wealth and output of the society trebled over night without any changes in its relative distribution among individuals. Would the issue of lessening inequality among those above the minimum subsistence level appear any less urgent? The answer can hardly be in the affirmative in view of the fact that the issue has grown more disturbing in the last hundred years despite the very great increases in productivity that have occurred. But the negative answer is curious. It initially appears that what is involved is envy, the dissatisfactions produced in men not by what they lack but by what others have. Josiah Wedgwood in his book on inheritance argues that:

in the search for material welfare, our modern civilization under conditions of industrial progress is continually manufacturing new and previously unwanted sources of pleasure, so that the old luxuries become the new necessities, alike for those who can and for those who cannot afford them. Hence where there is a great inequality of purchasing power, a continuous increase in the statistical total of goods and services produced per head will no doubt enable a larger and larger proportion of the people to satisfy certain wants, but will, equally certainly, increase the number of wants which the marjority desire to satisfy, and only the minority can.[183]

If this is what is primarily involved, the remedy, however impractical, would seem to be the one suggested by Aristotle that it is the desires of men and not their possessions that need be equalized. Nor is there much basis for optimism about the impact on envy of the redistribution of material goods. Every experience seems to confirm the dismal hypothesis that envy will find other, and possibly less attractive, places in which to take root.[184]

No proponent of progression has rested his case for doing something about economic inequality on the grounds of mitigating greed and envy. Basically two lines of argument for the coercive reduction of inequality

[183] Wedgwood, The Economics of Inheritance 14 (1929). Virtually the same observation is offered by David McCord Wright as an objection to the assumption that money has declining utility. Income Redistribution Reconsidered, in Income, Employment and Publication Policy: Essays in Honor of Alvin Hansen 159, 161 (1948).

[184] The study of the nursery is suggestive in this respect. "As between brothers and sisters, the first demand is to receive no less than they: this desire may be called the Communistic principle of the nursery. Every child is anxious to obtain the same share of food, of toys, of love, as the others; he is extremely envious of preferential treatment, and this jealousy is in no way proportional to his real needs." Bienenfeld, Rediscovery of Justice 19 (1947).

above the minimum subsistence level have been advanced and these may be complementary. One enlarges upon the improvements in the general welfare expected to result from greater economic equality;[185] the other examines the injustices as between individuals in permitting the existing degree of inequality to remain undisturbed.

The most prevalent form of the general welfare argument is that reducing inequality would tend to maximize economic welfare and, in Dalton's phrase, to prevent "considerable waste of potential economic welfare."[186] It is urged that the wealthy will lose less welfare by surrendering a share of their income than the less wealthy will gain by getting it. If the state is concerned with maximizing the happiness of its citizens, redistribution would then seem to be called for. This seems a highly persuasive position until one detects in it the motif of the minimum sacrifice theory. It will then be noted that the argument is once again enmeshed in considerations of whether money has a declining utility. No one would deny that making the less wealthy more wealthy would, if nothing else were involved, tend to produce an improvement in the general welfare. But in a coerced redistribution there is always the offsetting cost in the impact upon those whose incomes are being reduced; and there seems no way of holding that this offset would be less than one hundred per cent without in some form relying on the assumption that money has a declining utility curve which is roughly comparable for all men.

There is a further difficulty with such argument. The general welfare is stated in deceptively simple terms. Let us for the moment grant all the necessary assumptions about declining utility of money and agree that greater economic equality would bring about a net increase in the aggregate happiness of the individuals in the community. No matter how the case is put, it is still true that all that has happened is that the welfare of one group in the society has been increased at the expense of the welfare of a different group. Stated this way there is no "general" welfare; there is only the welfare of the two groups and the wealthy receive no counterbalancing benefits for their surrender of income or wealth. The welfare

[185] The most generalized form of the general welfare approach may be that which Fagan offers as his special analysis of the case for progression. Under it progression would be tested against all the "objective criteria of welfare," of which one, among others, may be the reduction of inequality. He offers this merely as a prospectus for future analysis and does not indicate whether progression would pass the test. The tenor of this approach is suggested by the following: "[C]onflicts between objective criteria, e.g., better housing versus less leisure, and conflicts of individual interest, e.g., more leisure for Jones versus less leisure for Smith, must be settled by inter-subjective agreement reached by free citizens under political conditions most conducive to the plasticity and mutuality of individual interests." Fagan, Recent and Contemporary Theories of Progressive Taxation, 46 J. Pol. Econ. 457, 497 (1938).

[186] Dalton, Some Aspects of Inequality of Incomes in Modern Communities 10 (1935).

argument is thus placed in a precarious position. If the wealthy have otherwise valid claims to their income, there is little reason for subordinating those claims to this narrow version of general welfare.

The argument is not basically altered when, in normative terms, it is stated that the government or the less wealthy would spend the money in a more desirable way than the rich. It would be a better society, it is said, if more were spent on housing and beer and less on yachts and champagne. Every man is entitled to his own views on what are the better and worse forms of consumption. But it is at least arguable that the brave new world would be even better if the less wealthy were given the additional money by the government without any strings attached and without any sumptuary restrictions. This is not to deny that in some matters collective expenditures by the government, as for parks, roads and police, are more efficacious than random expenditures of like amounts by individuals. While the advantages of such collective expenditures frequently have been associated with mitigating economic inequalities, and particularly so in socialist literature, this need not be the case. It obviously is possible and meaningful to finance the collective expenditures by a proportionate tax. In the end what may be appealing is not the way in which the less wealthy are spending the money but simply the fact that they, rather than the more wealthy, are spending it.[187]

---

[187] Even among those who favor measures to lessen economic inequality, there is a fundamental cleavage as to whether the increase in welfare is to be found in the fact that the less wealthy have relatively more money to spend or in the fact that the state is spending more money and will spend it more wisely. Thus Simons strongly favored redistribution but equally strongly opposed any increase in sumptuary spending by government. On the other hand, Tawney, a most enthusiastic advocate of equality, thought that only by collective expenditures could the redistribution of economic goods be made significant and could dissipation in driblets be avoided. Some thoughtful arguments for maximizing welfare by collective expenditures in certain situations are offered by Pigou in Economics of Welfare Pt. V, c. XI and c. I, IV (1920).

Wright has suggested that, as a practical matter, government expenditures must accompany redistribution, and argues that this is a net disadvantage. "One easily visualizes wealth redistribution as taking money from rich people and giving it to poor people. But this is true only in a very sophisticated sense. Money collected does not go directly to the poor—it goes to the government. It does not directly build up the poor—it builds up the government. The poor do not so often get purchasing power which they can spend as they wish, as services which they may not want. Nor do they get the full benefit of the taxes, but the taxes minus deductions (and possible wastage) for government service." Wright, op. cit. supra note 183, at 166.

Jewkes, in commenting on economic conditions in England under the Labour Government, concludes that "[i]t is a fair guess that the British consumer, taking everything together, is about in his prewar position. But there is one important qualification to that statement: to an increasing degree the consumer finds that his income is being spent for him by the state." Jewkes, Socialism's Legacy to Churchill, Fortune 79 (Dec. 1951).

Carver regarded such loss of consumer freedom as posing a dilemma for the serious equalitarian. Carver, The Ethical Basis of Distribution and Its Application to Taxation, 6 Annals 79, 85 (1895).

The general welfare argument has frequently been advanced beyond this stage of minimum sacrifice theory by pointing out the advantages to the community as a whole which would result from redistribution. One form of such argument has already been examined in detail in the earlier discussion of the relation of progression to the problem of economic instability. It will be recalled that on one view the bringing about of a more equal distribution of income was considered a good because of its hoped-for impact on the propensity of the society to consume; and that on another view a more equal distribution of income was regarded as a good because of its hoped-for impact on stability in the future. The limitations of these approaches to equality need not be restated.[188]

The community welfare approach to equality has also been couched in political terms. Democratic deliberation and decision, it has been urged, cannot operate as intended if there is too great a disparity in the wealth of the citizens.[189] Events of the last two decades have indelibly underscored the paramount importance of the basic political freedoms. It may well be that empty stomachs do not take the rights of free speech, assembly and franchise very seriously. It may be true that increases in economic power spell increases in political power and that in effect the rich man can vote more than once. And it may be that there are limits to the peaceful tolerance by the mass of the population of great disparities in wealth and that a closer approximation to equality is important insurance against revolution.[190] But at least in our society there are many routes to political power, and money appears not to be the most significant of these. In a complex society some considerable differentials in political power are bound to exist, and money may well be less unpleasant and rigid than such other routes as heredity, social caste, or military prestige. Particularly in a democratic society it may be important to keep open the money route to power since it provides needed checks and competition for other avenues depending more on status.[191] In any event all of the arguments for lessen-

---

[188] See text, section 7 supra.

[189] This is a recurring theme in Tawney, Equality (1929). The Lasswell and McDougal essay on legal education is suggestive of relationships between "balanced income" and the basic democratic values. Lasswell and McDougal, Legal Education and Public Policy: Profession Training in the Public Interest, 52 Yale L.J. 203 (1943).

[190] But note Edgeworth's observation: "This levelling principle requires to be corrected by several prudential considerations. . . . [T]here is the danger of awakening the predatory instinct of the poor, and precipitating revolution." II Edgeworth, Papers Relating to Political Economy 130 (1925).

[191] "Judged from the viewpoint of choosing among alternate forms of rivalry rather than eliminating it entirely, capitalist competition and income incentives are submitted to compare much more favorably. Two main standards must be noted: democracy of life and aspiration, and technological creativeness. While the analysis . . . could be carried to denial of the

ing equality for political reasons lose a good deal of their force when taken
to be arguments for lessening the inequality of those above the minimum
subsistence level.

A closely associated contention is that money represents economic
power which permits its owners to make economic decisions affecting the
lives of others.[192] It is argued that the possessor of any wealth is like a
private sovereign, and that great economic disparities result in comparable
disparities in the distribution of such "sovereign" power. By analogy to
the political sphere it is urged that economic inequality must be avoided
to avoid economic tyranny and to promote economic democracy. This line
of argument appears to confuse wealth with monopoly. It is true that a
monopolist can exercise economic power irresponsibly and take advantage
of others. It is not true that the owner of great wealth who is subject to the
discipline of competition has any such power. Moreover, the lessening of
economic inequalities is at best an oblique attack on monopoly and in
most situations the redistribution of income is not very likely to terminate
economic monopolies.

There are finally a cluster of observations about the increases in moral
and spiritual values which are said to result from reducing economic inequalities.[193] These points typically are stated with great eloquence but

---

value of material progress, we do not go so far. Mere gadgets will certainly never solve the
fundamental problem of the true and the beautiful. But increasing technical efficiency reduces
the amount of personally degrading labor, increases health, and, as a matter of history, has
been accompanied by increasing social conscience and reduction of caste barriers.

"Yet material progress is not a matter of mere 'extension'—not simply making 'more of the
same.' I find my chief sanction for the competitive order in what may be called the 'Law of
Deterioration of Self-perpetuating Groups.' Where access to the top is conditioned on the
consent of those already there, promotion is likely to go to the agreeable conformist rather
than the able explorer. The group in power increasingly surrounds itself with yes men. The
caliber of the 'palace guard' rapidly declines." Wright, op. cit. supra note 183, at 168.

[192] See, e.g., Tawney, Equality 210–18 (1929). But compare Wright's pessimism about
the results of redistribution carried out through government: "Liberals, particularly in this
country, have advocated high progressive income taxes with the largely unconscious, or un-
expressed, mental assumption that that is the way to get a nation of many middle-sized, independent businesses and many middle-class independent people. But this assumption does not
automatically fulfill itself. We may well get instead a nation whose economic life is carried on
by the state, or by a few corporations owned or controlled by the state; and a population not
of independent middle-class owners, but of dependent clerks and government employees. The
flow of money and resources into government hands, and hence the power of the state, is
directly increased without being at all sure that any reciprocal, or proportionately reciprocal,
benefits will be forthcoming to the individual." Wright, op. cit. supra note 183, at 167.

[193] But compare: "I would rather say that it is dangerous to get too much interested in
equality. Groups then form with a great development of fellow-feeling that is found in the
supporters of dictators. They all say they are just alike. They are part of the crowd; they lose
themselves in it; they do not differentiate; they do not have rewards or competition. Competition, among other things, may draw off a lot of the impulses that lead to war." Sharp, What
Is Equality?, Univ. Chi. Round Table No. 412 (Loomer, Sharp, Singer) 16 (1946).

are difficult to pin down analytically. Thus R. H. Tawney, who is a leading spokesman in this connection, says:

What is repulsive is not that one man should earn more than others, for where
community of environment, and common education and a habit of life have bred a
common tradition of respect and consideration, these details of the counting-house
are forgotten or ignored. It is that some classes should be excluded from the heritage
of civilization which others enjoy, and that the fact of human fellowship, which is
ultimate and profound, should be obscured by economic contrasts, which are trivial
and superficial.[194]

Or again:

Men are, in great measure, what they feel themselves to be, and they think of themselves as they are thought of by their fellows. The advance in individual self-respect
and in social amenity caused by the softening of the more barbarous inequalities of
the past is a contribution to civilization as genuine as the improvement in material
conditions.[195]

We can all agree that it would be better to have a society in which men
respected the basic dignity of their fellow men, in which there were few
barriers to human relations, and in which it was universally realized that
man does not live by bread alone. The only question is whether the lessening of economic inequalities among those above the minimum subsistence
level can make a significant contribution to bringing about such a society. Money differences are only one of a long list of factors that divide
men from one another in our society, and it is quite possible that as differences in income were lessened other differences with more unpleasant
overtones would become more important.[196] This of course is not to contend that economic inequality is itself a good.[197] It is rather only to sound a
skeptical note as to how much moral reform will be effected by this type of
economic change.

[194] Tawney, Equality 139–40 (1929).

[195] Ibid., at 171.

[196] "One such standard is the idea that virtual income equality helps remove envy, rivalry,
conflict, and frustration from economic life. But what is gained by eliminating rivalry for
income if rivalry for power or prestige remain? Sparsely settled communities of meditating
ascetics might have no government and no rivalry. But an integrated machine economy, even
if the 'state' has 'withered,' implies a hierarchy of technical operatives, and enough ambition
must survive for men to *want* responsible operative positions. . . .

"[S]upposing we conclude it desirable to give at least some responsibility to those most
competent in their respective fields, a problem of selection immediately appears. But those
not selected may feel hurt. The argument against income difference, *per se*, closes its eyes to
the profundity of the problem of frustration as we find it in our universe. . . ." Wright, op. cit.
supra note 183, at 162–63.

[197] In the past it was often argued that a wealthy group was needed to be the sponsors and
carriers of culture in the society. Sidgwick, The Principles of Political Economy 524 et seq.
(2d ed., 1887). But as literacy and education become more universal this point loses much of
whatever force it may have had.

17

The discussion of redistribution as a justification for progression has up to this point considered only one side of the matter—the advantages of redistribution to the recipients and to the whole community. Men will of course assess these advantages variously. While the advantages are less determinate than might have been anticipated, it is clear that at worst they are neutral and do not suggest a substantial argument against lessening inequality. But, inasmuch as redistribution involves the compulsory taking of income from the more wealthy, it is necessary to examine their claim to the income which is proposed to be taken from them under progression.[197a] It is this part of the case for progression which is likely to be most challenging and disturbing. If the original distribution is found to be less than fair this indictment may provide a substantial new argument, perhaps a decisive one, for progression. But if the original distribution is found to be fair the case for progression on grounds of redistribution runs into a heavy counterbalancing injustice. The whole issue is made more acute when examined within the confines of a commitment to a system of private enterprise and property.[198]

The most obvious complaint about the market in its allocation of rewards is that the market never works according to the Adam Smith blueprint. It is clear that there are numerous distorting elements. Monopoly in various forms exists and there is no doubt that in many areas it is of serious magnitude. It of course produces a pattern of distribution which

[197a] In a recent survey of the attitudes of ministers on social problems, the following question was put: "Some observers say a steeply graduated income tax violates the moral principle that man is entitled to the fruits of his labor. How do you feel about this?" The responses were distributed in this manner:

Disagree	71%
Agree	10%
Qualified	15%
No Opinion	4%

Johnson, The Preacher Speaks on Social Problems, 3 Faith and Freedom 3 (1952).

[198] "In the last analysis, whether or not one believes that the progressive principle is desirable depends considerably upon his general philosophy of life. In this respect people are generally divisible into two groups. One group would prefer a world in which a free hand is given to the strong and the clever. This group holds that a free struggle makes for strong, vigorous character and that large inequalities are necessary to support the economic incentives. These people accept the progressive principle, if at all, with reluctance. They feel that progressive taxation, especially if the rates are steeply graduated, violates the moral law against one's 'reaping where he has not sown.' They also contend that many who wish the tax system to reduce inequalities would confine its role in this respect to incomes above their own. The second group holds that the strong have a decided obligation to the weak and stresses the solidarity of human interests. It dislikes and doubts the wisdom of great inequalities. Those who belong to this latter group are very likely to approve the progressive principle with enthusiasm." Groves, Financing Government 49–50 (rev. ed., 1945).

deviates from that projected by market theory. There are also the disturbing influences of fraud and duress which affect the distribution of rewards and which have not been and cannot be perfectly policed. Another factor is the periodic shifts in the value of money and in the level of economic activity which have had a pronounced impact on the distribution pattern. And there is always the element of sheer luck or chance which sometimes is the best explanation of success or failure. Taking these factors together there undoubtedly is a large amount of "undeserved" income distributed by our contemporary market system. By itself, however, this does not establish a case for redistribution of income through progression.

One long-standing objection to the use of progression to correct these imperfections of the system has been that it deals with effects and not causes.[199] To the extent a progressive tax system might operate to lessen concern with the direct enforcement of the antitrust laws, for example, the objection has force. But surely even with a much more forceful attack on the causes, significant distortion would still remain.

Of greater importance is the difficulty of correlating the "undeserved" income with the rates under a progressive schedule. To obtain such correlation it is necessary that there be some general relationship between total income and undeserved income and that the undeserved component increase more rapidly than the total income. Almost nothing is known about the distribution of undeserved income, and guesses about its probable distribution seem to be a most precarious base on which to rest the tax structure. Nearly a hundred years ago Mill pointed out that attempting to correct for undeserved income by a general progressive tax would be unconscionably crude.

It is unlikely, however, that the feeling for the greater justice of more equal distribution rests primarily on the implicit criticism of the accuracy or adequacy of the market mechanism in distributing rewards.[200] Even if it were thought that the market was freed of all restraints and was working

[199] "Progressive taxation, so far as it aims to correct unjustified inequalities, evidently deals with results, not causes. It is obviously better to go to the root of the matter, and to deal with the causes. Much the more effective and promising way of reform is to promote the mitigation of inequality in other ways—by equalization of opportunity through widespread facilities for rational education, by the control of monopoly industries, by the removal of the conditions which make possible illegitimate profits. Progressive taxation, which deals with income (or property) solely according to size, and not according to social desert, is less discriminating and also less effective in reaching the ultimate goal than the various other ways of spreading material welfare." 2 Taussig, Principles of Economics 492 (1911). To the same effect is Adams, Science of Finance 335 (1898). Compare Fagan, Recent and Contemporary Theories of Progressive Taxation, 46 J. Pol. Econ. 457, 495 n. 80 (1938).

[200] One other source of doubt about the distribution effectuated by the market—inequality of opportunity—is discussed in the text, section 18 infra.

perfectly, many would be uneasy about substantial disparities in rewards. Thus it is necessary to probe more deeply why there is a persistent attractiveness to the justice of greater economic equality among individuals.

One possible explanation of this attitude may lie in an ultimate doubt about the rationality of any scheme of differential rewards.[201] Presumably a rational scheme would be one that rewarded men for the achievements for which they were personally responsible. The great question is to what extent men are responsible for their differences. It has long been explicitly recognized that this is a most troublesome question when the companion problem of punishment is considered. The same factors which have become so familiar in stirring doubts as to how to deal with the criminal— the inborn endowment, the lack of opportunities, and the unfortunate environment for the development of the personality—make one hesitant to conclude that men are entitled to their rewards any more than to their punishments. From this perspective everyone's income is equally undeserved, and the market, however important its other functions,[202] is an amoral distributor of rewards. If one confesses to knowing nothing about who is entitled to the goods of the world then the most prudent and sensible thing to do is count each man as one.

It may well be true that if one fully rejects the notion of any personal deservedness of rewards, "[w]e may plead, remonstrate, preach, and exhort; but we cannot prove."[203] Nevertheless the riddle of personal responsibility is not easily put to rest. Whatever we may think in moments of tranquility, we do not live from day to day without the help of the assumption that those around us and we ourselves deserve in some way the praise and blame, the rewards and punishments, we all dispense and receive.[204] To most of us most of the time, a praiseworthy man is not simply an

[201] Simons had this doubt. "At any rate, it may be best to start by denying any justification for prevailing inequality in terms of personal desert. This position has the great virtue of being definite; and it seems more nearly defensible than any other simple position relevant to the immediate problem." Simons, Personal Income Taxation 18 (1938).

[202] A sufficient justification for employing a market system may be found in its advantages as a way of organizing economic life with a minimum of coercion, a maximum of individual freedom of choice, and as a form of insurance against making "great" errors. See Knight, The Meaning of Freedom, 52 Ethics 86 (1940).

[203] Simons, Personal Income Taxation 18 (1938).

[204] The nursery is again suggestive on this score. "Nevertheless, ardently as every child clamours for equality of treatment, and later of status, he desires just as fiercely to be rewarded for his endeavours and his achievements. . . . It is but human that the child should on the one hand take offense at the preference shown to his fellows as a reward for their endeavors, and, on the other, be equally offended if some special success of his own remains unrewarded." Bienenfeld, Rediscovery of Justice 20 (1947). Cf. note 184 supra.

aesthetically remarkable object of nature, like a beautiful sunset. And the very psychological insights which in recent years have made us aware how little we control ourselves have also pointed up how achievement depends on a factor for which we might be said to be responsible. No matter what our endowments of heredity and environment, something more is required for them to be realized, and this something must be close to the heart of personal responsibility. For fulfillment, even the most lavish talents require perseverance, discipline, integrity, dedication and other personal qualities. There are at least two reasons, not just one, why most of us do not play the violin as well as Heifetz. It may be that personal responsibility is just one more inherited talent, but even so it is still uniquely appealing to tie our system of rewards and punishments to it.[204a]

A second possible explanation of the predilection for greater economic equality may be found in the fact of the division of labor.[205] In all economies, and particularly in the modern economy, any man's production requires the cooperation of many others. Because all of these efforts are indispensable to the final product it has seemed to some not possible to differentiate, except arbitrarily, between the contributions of each to the final result. Here, as in many other problems of life, baseball affords a useful analogy. The whole squad, including the all-star center fielder and the rookie relief pitcher, are equally indispensable; and no player, not even Cobb, Ruth or DiMaggio, wins games by himself. The thrust of the point is that there is no way of isolating the contribution of any player; or at least that any differential pricing of services should be subject to substantial reduction in recognition of the contribution made by the team itself. But this view of the pricing process overstates the ambiguity arising out of the division of labor. The pricing process does separate out the value to society of the various component services, taking account of the scarcity of each type of service and the demand for it. If it is agreed that the

---

[204a] Cannan, in a striking passage about the inequality of income from labor, puts himself the question, "What should a person do in order to get good earnings . . . ?" He begins his answer in a light vein by noting that it is advisable to choose suitable parents, to be born a boy rather than a girl, and to select a suitable occupation. But then he goes on to say: "Once in his occupation, he must be industrious and as efficient as possible. The idlers, the fools, and other good-for-nothings will tell him it is no use, that the standard wage will be paid him anyway, and that promotion goes entirely by seniority or favouritism, but he must treat them as the liars they are, and hold to the belief that though there are unlucky exceptions, yet as a rule the industrious and efficient do better than the lazy and the inefficient." Cannan, A Review of Economic Theory 388–89 (1929).

[205] See Hobhouse, The Elements of Social Justice 162–63 (1921); Groves, Financing Government 39 (rev. ed., 1945).

individual is sufficiently responsible for his scarce talent, it should not be disturbing to reward him for his distinctive achievement and contribution.[206]

A third possible explanation may be derived from special skepticism about the narrowness of economic rewards even though they are based on an accurate measure of achievement. The source of the difficulty is that economic achievement is not the total of human accomplishment; there is more to a man than that which the market can appraise or reward, and there is thus an inevitable discrepancy between the "pricing" of the whole man and the pricing of his economic talents by the market. This is not to argue that the market rewards the wrong talents and that therefore the market should be abolished as the arbiter of rewards.[207] Rather it is to emphasize that the market does not purport to take all qualities fully into account. Consequently we are tempted to second-guess the market either by giving recognition to some qualities which the market ignores or by discounting some qualities which it almost inadvertently seems to overrate. On the one hand, we may be troubled that the society may tend to rate the whole man by his income and hence we may seek some way of blunting the finality of the market's rating of men. Or, on the other hand, we may be impressed with the extraordinary power and versatility of the monetary reward. It is so desirable a reward that we would like to bring it into play in rating the whole man.[208]

Regardless of how this point is put we are impressed with the importance of the society's retaining the power to review and adjust the distribution of income and wealth which its market and its laws bring about. We rebel at any notion that the society is foreclosed from second-guessing the market. The ultimate appeal of the progressive tax may then be that it is the only attractive way of doing this without interfering too much with the operation of the market. Progression then would be an assurance by the society that the answers of the market were not taken with absolute finality.

This defense of progression has some rather strict limits. In its most

[206] The baseball analogy is suggestive in one further respect. If a team wins a pennant, it is the universally followed rule that the prize money is distributed *equally* among all who have been members of the squad throughout the season.

[207] It has of course not been universally agreed that the traits the market principally rewards are virtues. One writer has described the market as rewarding enterprisers for "unamiable and non-socially desirable traits of character, such as acquisitiveness, narrowness of intellectual and social outlook, and dominant self assertion." Peck, Taxation and Welfare 200 (1925).

[208] The economic market is not the only appraiser and rewarder in our society. Fortunately there in effect are "noneconomic markets" for noneconomic qualities of man. In areas such as those concerned with personal friendships, it is certainly true that virtue is its own reward.

plausible form it reduces the tax to a kind of ceremonial commitment and nothing more. At best this would justify a very mild degree of progression. But even after stating that progression has a ceremonial value, one cannot be sure what the reach of the point really is. Certainly it is not made articulate by any large segment of the public, nor is it an explicit political creed, nor is it a theory of the experts. Moreover it clearly is an after-the-fact explanation, since, if a progressive tax were not already in operation, it is almost inconceivable that anyone would advocate introducing one on this ground. Nevertheless it perhaps is as close as we can come to detecting what it is about the tax that remains so persistently attractive on grounds of individual justice: It is a sort of last refuge for doing something politely about the distribution of income under a market system.[209]

If such speculations come close to the source of the appeal of progression they also underscore why there has been so little frank discussion of progression on grounds of minimizing economic inequalities. The lingering fear must always have been that any case for progression on these grounds proves too much. It has been seen that it is quite difficult to sponsor progression on the basis of economic equality without calling into question either the meaningfulness of personal responsibility or the fairness with which the market distributes rewards. Progression, when offered on these grounds, is an unsettling idea.

18

There is still another road leading to the problem of equality. Almost everybody professes to be in favor of one kind of equality—equality of opportunity. What remains to be investigated is the relationship between this kind of equality and economic equality.

Equality of opportunity might well have been discussed in connection with both the general welfare approach to equality and the arguments concerning rewards. While consideration of equality of opportunity has been isolated here as a matter of convenience, neither the previous discussion of general welfare nor that of rewards can be taken as complete without some reference to it. In terms of the justice of rewards, the point is that no race can be fair unless the contestants start from the same mark. Tawney said:

If the rules of a game give a permanent advantage to some of the players, it does not become fair merely because they are scrupulously observed by all who take part in it. When the contrast between the circumstances of different social strata is so profound

[209] It is at least arguable that such a ceremony may prove to be self-defeating, since in its efforts to de-emphasize the importance of money differentials it necessarily invites attention to them. But compare Galbraith, American Capitalism 187–88 (1952).

as today, the argument—if it deserves to be called an argument—which suggests that the income they receive bears a close relation to their personal qualities is obviously illusory.[210]

In general welfare terms, the relevance of inequalities of opportunity is that without equal opportunity for individuals to develop their talents society will be deprived of the full use of its potential human resources. In this sense equality of opportunity is viewed as a sufficient good in itself and not as a way of correcting for distortions in the allocation of rewards by the market. For all practical purposes it makes little difference whether equality of opportunity is approached by one of these routes or the other. Whatever can be said about it will in the main be relevant under both approaches.

It might simplify matters somewhat to go directly to the heart of the problem—the children. While there is still a flickering interest in eugenics, the concern today is not with lessening hereditary inequalities. We now realize that so little is known about human heredity[211] that we never get to the hard question whether we would be willing to put into practice our knowledge of heredity. Nor is the problem today one of removing explicit legal barriers; even in the area of racial discrimination these scarcely exist in our society.[212] The important inequalities of opportunity are inequalities of environment, in its broadest sense, for the children. It is the inequalities in the worlds which the children inherit which count, and this inheritance is both economic and cultural.

The inheritance of wealth at death is of course an old and familiar topic in itself. The controversies over it need not be reviewed at length here. It need only be noted that the basic argument for levelling such inheritances is simply the case for equality of opportunity among the children, and today few dispute the force of the equalitarian case in this context. On the other hand the impairment of incentives to work and to accumulate and the disruption of the family standard of living are not without considerable force or familiarity as counterbalancing arguments against too severely limiting the inheritance of wealth.

For our purposes it can be safely concluded that the case for lessening inequalities in such inheritance is surely stronger than the case for lessening inequalities of income. The windfall aspect of inheritance clearly

---

[210] Equality 143–44 (1929). For a somewhat different point of view see Mellon, Taxation: The People's Business 12 (1924): "Any man of energy and initiative in this country can get what he wants out of life."

[211] See Cook, Eugenics or Euthenics, 37 Ill. L. Rev. 287 (1943).

[212] In recent years the most explicit analysis of the many facets of equality of opportunity has been made in connection with the efforts to remove racial barriers; see for example McIver, The More Perfect Union (1948).

distinguishes the two cases. Moreover there is a tradition of favoring a progressive tax on inheritance but a proportionate tax on income.[213] In any event the progressive income tax is certainly not a direct equivalent of a progressive inheritance tax.[214] An inheritance tax reaches accumulated wealth; an income tax, while it may retard further accumulations of wealth, can only reach the income from existing wealth and not the wealth itself. It thus performs the primary function of an inheritance tax only to the limited extent that it prevents disparities in wealth from growing.

But this interpretation of the role of the income tax misses the most suggestive part of the relationship between the case for a progressive inheritance tax and the case for a progressive income tax. Looking only at the inequality involved in some children inheriting wealth at the death of kin and other children inheriting no wealth ignores the more far-reaching instances of economic discriminations among children. These can most easily be pointed up where the parents survive until the children have reached adulthood. In such situations the critical economic inheritance occurs prior to the death of the parents and need not be related to the wealth, if any, which they pass on directly at death or by way of inter vivos gifts of wealth. The critical economic inheritance consists of the day to day expenditures on the children; it is these expenditures which add up to money investments in the children's health, education and welfare which in the aggregate are, at least in our society, gravely disparate. No progressive inheritance tax, or combination of gift and inheritance taxes, can touch this source of economic inequalities among children.[215] On the other hand a progressive income tax can, as one of its effects, help to minimize this form of unequal inheritance. It is income, not wealth, which is the important operative factor here, and by bringing incomes closer together the tax tends to bring money investments in children closer together.[216]

[213] Mill is a famous example of this combination. See his Principles of Political Economy Bk. 2, c. 2 and Bk. 5, c. 2 (Ashley's ed., 1923). By a tax on inheritance we mean any form of death transfer tax.

[214] The point is that a tax on annual income in the ordinary sense does not perform the same functions as a tax on transfers of wealth. It would be possible, as Simons urged, to treat inheritance and inter vivos transfers as income to the recipients under the regular income tax. Personal Income Taxation c. 6 (1938).

[215] Under our present tax system the expenditures made by parents in bringing up children are almost completely excluded from consideration. The expenditures are not treated as income to the children or as gifts made by the parents. Moreover the gift tax has allowed, in addition to the relatively large basic exemption for the donor, a substantial annual exclusion for each donee.

[216] It might be noted that a tax on inheritance also serves to bring incomes closer together.

But the gravest source of inequality of opportunity in our society is not economic but rather what is called cultural inheritance for lack of a better term. Under modern conditions the opportunities for formal education, healthful diet and medical attention to some extent can be equalized by economic means without too greatly disrupting the family. However, it still remains true that even today much of the transmission of culture, in the narrow sense, occurs through the family, and no system of public education and training can completely neutralize this form of inheritance. Here it is the economic investment in the parents and the grandparents, irrevocably in the past, which produces differential opportunities for the children. Nor is this the end of the matter. It has long been recognized that the parents make the children in their own image, and modern psychology has served to underscore how early this process begins to operate and how decisive it may be. The more subtle and profound influences upon the child resulting from love, integrity and family morale form a kind of inheritance which cannot, at least for those above the minimum subsistence level, be significantly affected by economic measures, or possibly by any others. If these influences on the members of the next generation are to be equalized, nothing short of major changes in the institution of the family can possibly suffice.[217] At a minimum such changes would include socializing decisions not only about how children are to be raised but who is to raise them. And this in turn would call into question the very having of children.

19

In examining equality our concern has been with the relationship between the broad case for economic equality and the special case for the progressive income tax. More specifically, attention has been directed to what is implied in advocating progression on grounds of reducing economic inequalities within a set of commitments to the privacy of the family, the ownership of private property, and the existence of the market as the principal method of organizing economic life. Since the case for progression on equality grounds is ultimately the case for equality itself, it is not surprising that no definitive assessment of this line of justification for progression

[217] "A human being, as a person and a member of society, has needs and rights which are ignored and flouted when he is taken economically as a datum. He has rights to be and to have which it is absurd and monstrous to take as defined and measured by his productive capacity, which is so largely beyond his control. Obviously, the family is much more real as a social-economic unit than is the literal, biological individual, and the problems center more in the family, and the various forms of inheritance, than in the relations between individuals." Knight, The Meaning of Freedom, 52 Ethics 86 (1940). See also Knight, The Ideal of Freedom: Conditions for Its Realization, in The Philosophy of American Democracy (Perry ed., 1943) 87, 115 et seq.

can be made. Certain fairly definite observations do however suggest themselves.[218]

The thing that most clearly emerges is that the case for mitigating economic inequalities is a different case when the reference is to adults than when it is to children. As to adults both the justification for reducing inequalities and the possibility of doing something significant about them are in question. The basic concern is not with levels of real income but with relative incomes. In this respect, whether the argument for redistributing income is put in terms of increasing the general welfare or of redressing the injustice of the existing rewards, it is always precariously close to being rested simply on envy. Furthermore, when the argument is stated in general welfare terms there is difficulty in finding improvements in the welfare of the whole community and not just in the welfare of the immediate recipients of the redistribution. And when it is stated in terms of rewards, the argument is always dangerously near to proving too much about the irrationality or narrowness of rewards, or about the unfairness of the market system as an allocator of rewards.

In the case of children these difficulties largely disappear. There is an enormously stronger ethical claim to equality for the sake of children. What may reduce to envy as among adults surely is justice as among children; the contribution to the general welfare which comes from equalizing opportunities among the children is also compelling; and the majority of the doubts about the fairness of a competitive system of rewards would be put to rest if the start of the race were thus equalized.

There are however other difficulties if the society is insistent about equalizing opportunities among children. It soon becomes apparent that the deepest cultural inequalities to which children are heirs cannot be reached short of reforms which would force us far beyond our commitment to the privacy of the family and perhaps to the institution of private property. But even the half loaf has difficulties of its own. It has been pointed out, by David McCord Wright for example, that as long as there continues to be a substantial amount of wealth passing privately from one

[218] It may be relevant at this point to revisit McCulloch's objection about the uncertainty of the rate pattern under progression. See text, section 10 supra. Is the objection as forceful if the rates are set primarily with a view to lessening inequality rather than with a view to equalizing sacrifice? The answer appears clearly to be no. In the case of sacrifice analysis, because of the nature of the data it is quite possible for those who set the rates to err and fail to equalize sacrifice. While perhaps no two men will agree as to how much equality they desire, presumably neither man is making an error in applying his preference. If their preferences are not equally sound, that is a matter for democratic debate to resolve. In the end the distrust of progression on grounds of the uncertainty of the equality standard is only a doubt about the wisdom of entrusting the question of economic equality to the democratic process. See section 5 (b).

generation to the next, a progressive income tax decreases the opportunity for new accumulations of comparable wealth.[219] And this in turn may result in the evils of a self-perpetuating elite. Even in the absence of significant private inheritance, and so long as the state itself does not undertake to raise all the children, the equalizing of opportunity may turn out to be circular. If the incomes of parents are subjected to a substantially progressive tax for the sake of equalizing the opportunities of the children, there will be a dilemma when the children grow up. If their incomes are not subject to such a tax, the inequalities of opportunities will reappear among their children. But if their incomes are subject to such levelling by taxation, they will be denied the opportunity to enjoy the differential rewards which they have earned. In effect we would be first making certain that the conditions for the race are fair and then calling the race off.[220]

In the end what perhaps emerges most strongly from a consideration of equality and progression is that, in approaching economic inequality via taxation of income, one is most easily permitted to endorse greater economic equality as a goal without having to face point blank the perplexities of the equality issue.[221]

20

Since even the proponents of a proportionate tax generally are willing to concede the need for an exemption for those below the minimum sub-

[219] Wright, op. cit. supra note 183, at 167.

[220] There is at least another sense in which equality of opportunity is self-defeating. "Nearly two centuries ago Dr. Johnson declaimed against the ideal of equality of opportunity. He argued that permitting ambition in everyone would greatly increase unhappiness—for only a few could be at the top in any generation. Following this line, it could be maintained that the idea of relatively equal *opportunity* is a self-defeating one. The more nearly it is attained the less will those who do not rise be prepared to admit the inevitable implication regarding themselves, and the more fiercely will they try to blame their personal failures upon 'the system.' " Wright, op. cit. supra note 183, at 171.

[221] One objection which haunts the literature on equality should here be noted. It is frequently urged that redistribution will be futile since even a literal equalization of wealth and income would add so little to each of the many beneficiaries. As a matter of cold mathematics this is undoubtedly true, even ignoring the adverse impact on productivity. But this does not make the lessening of economic inequality a trivial thing. To the extent the reduction of inequality is a matter of relative rather than real incomes, this objection misses the point altogether. To the extent that the redistribution is intended to correct for what is conceived to be the injustice of the existing distribution, the objection again misses the point. To the extent that the concern is with lessening the inequalities of opportunity for the children, once again the objection falls.

Finally, even where the concern is with real income, the objection is subject to considerable qualification. By concentrating the benefits on the very poorest members of the community, the improvement of their economic position can be made substantial. And by distributing the benefits in the form of community expenditures, rather than cash, the substantiality of the benefits can, although not without offsetting disadvantages, be preserved.

sistence level, it might seem that the issue of exemptions is not relevant to an analysis of the merits of progression. In the discussion thus far care has been taken to exclude explicitly concern with those below the exemption level. However it was noted at the start of the essay that as a practical matter any exemption in an otherwise proportionate tax introduces an element of progression in the effective rates. It remains to examine whether the inevitability of this form of progression carries with it any implications for a general theory of progression.[222]

As a preliminary matter it is necessary to understand why there is practically no way of avoiding the progression that comes from an exemption. The central problem of an exemption, aside from determining its size, is deciding how it is to be handled with respect to persons who are above the exemption level. Fundamentally there are only three possible choices.[223] The first is to deny the exemption altogether to those above the exemption level. This has the difficulty of resulting in extremely high, if not absurdly high, marginal rates of tax on the dollars of income immediately above the exemption level. For example, assume that the exemption is $1,000 and that the flat rate of tax is 10%. If taxpayers with incomes above $1,000 are not allowed to deduct any part of the exemption, then a taxpayer with an income of $1,100 would pay a total tax of $110, which is a tax of 110% on his last hundred dollars. This result is so unfair and im-

---

[222] Exemptions have suggested at least one other line of defense for progression. A system of graduated rates can always be viewed as a graduated series of exemptions. This is most easily seen if it is imagined that new rate brackets are added at the top one at a time, as though they were a series of separate taxes each of which has its own exemption, and each new exemption being larger than the prior one. On this view there is then a flat tax (the top rate) and a series of exemptions graduated downward. Thus, the larger the income the smaller the exemption, and conversely. Gustav Cassel argued that the only proper meaning for exemption was indispensable income and that this increased as the income increased because as a social reality luxuries for the lower incomes become necessities for the upper incomes. Further, he thought that this nucleus of indispensable and untaxable income increased more slowly than the total income of individuals. Finally, he urged that the dispensable remainders of all incomes should be taxed at the same rate, on the grounds of equal sacrifice. From this it follows inevitably that a flat rate of tax on the nonexempt incomes results in a progressive tax on the whole incomes.

While this was a most ingenious effort, it gets its effect by changing the meaning of indispensable income. Indispensable is no longer defined in terms of sheer subsistence level but rather in terms of reliance on a customary standard of living at a given income level. Once this step is taken the proposal becomes a variant of sacrifice theory. Cassel, The Theory of Progressive Taxation, 11 Econ. J. 481 (1901).

[223] The three possibilities are clearly analyzed as lump sum, continuing, and vanishing exemptions in Shultz and Harriss, American Public Finance 261 et seq. (5th ed., 1949). The substitution of a credit against taxes in lieu of the exemption deduction is not really a fourth alternative since the primary carry-over effect of the exemption among taxpayers remains. The credit has been recommended simply to keep the value of the exemption from increasing as income and marginal rates increase. U.S. Treas. Dep't Study, Individual Income Tax Exemptions (1947).

practical that it is unlikely that any tax system would knowingly adopt it.[224]

The other two basic choices avoid this result by giving all or part of the benefit of the exemption to persons with incomes above the exemption level, although they may not be the intended beneficiaries of the exemption. One method, that developed by the English, consists of gradually eliminating the deduction of the exemption for those above the exemption level. This is accomplished by graduating the exemption inversely with the amount of income and in that way graduating the rate of tax. In this system there are three critical levels: the floor below which no tax is paid; the ceiling above which no deduction for an exemption is allowed; and the intermediate class of incomes which are subject to a tax explicitly graduated up to the ceiling level. Here the effort to adjust for the exemption by tapering it produces an explicitly progressive system, although within a limited range, and for a limited purpose.

The American solution has been to allow all taxpayers to deduct the same amount of exemption regardless of their total income. Coupled with a flat tax this solution also yields a progressive tax, but the mathematics are slightly more complicated. It is true that the marginal rate of tax is not graduated except in the sense that for all taxpayers below the exemption level it is zero. However the effective rates of tax on the total incomes of taxpayers vary from zero to (but never quite reaching) the single flat rate as a limit.

These are no minor mathematical truths. It is evident that the steepness of the progression which can be obtained by combining a flat tax and an exemption varies directly with the size of the exemption and the rate of the tax. At the initial rates of tax and with the exemptions to which we have become accustomed under our federal estate and income tax systems, a very substantial degree of progression exists entirely independently of the graduated rates.[225] Under the federal estate tax, for example, the effective exemption is $60,000; this means that with a gross estate of $120,000 the nominal tax rate is cut in half because only one-half the estate is subject to the rate; and with a gross estate as large as $600,000 the exemption has the effect of discounting the nominal rate by 10%.[226] For the bulk of taxable estates the exemption is a very significant factor in the

[224] There is a negligible set of notches in the personal income tax at present for taxpayers with gross incomes under $5,000 who elect to compute their tax from the tax tables. See Int. Rev. Code, Supp. T, 62 Stat. 129 (1948), 26 U.S.C.A. §401 (1951).

[225] This is also true of the gift tax.

[226] The marital deduction makes this progression much steeper since it in effect may double the size of the exemption.

actual progression of the tax. In the case of our federal income tax the exemption for the average married taxpayer is around $3,000.[227] With a first bracket rate of about 20%, it is easy to appreciate that the exemption produces a substantial degree of progression apart from the graduation of rates. In fact, for the majority of income taxpayers all or practically all of the progression is still that which is derived from the exemption and not from the graduation of rates.

If some progression is inescapable as a result of exemptions it might at first impression seem that the case for exemptions would give insight into the general case for progression. But this turns out not to be true.

Although practically an exemption must produce progression, there is nothing in the case for exemptions, powerful as it is, which lends support to a general theory of progression. The case for exemptions has been rested on the diseconomy of collecting small amounts of tax out of many low incomes; on the futility of the state giving welfare benefits with one hand and taxing the recipients with the other; and on the disadvantages of anchoring judgments about tax rates and government expenditures to the capacities of the poorest members of the community.[228] Whatever the strength of these considerations, they hardly have much relevance for a general theory of progression. It is true that the various justifications offered for progression can be adapted as even stronger justifications for fully exempting those below the minimum subsistence level. The clearest case of a difference, whether in the benefits received from government, or in the utility of money, or in inequalities of income, is found by comparing those below the minimum subsistence level with those above it. This however does not reach very far in supporting progression since one can always insist that he can draw a distinction at the minimum subsistence level but that he can draw no further ones among persons above that level.[229]

Again on first impression it might seem that, however different the case for exemptions and the case for general progression may be, an exemption once granted would produce a sufficient progression to obliterate any real

[227] The present system allows a $600 exemption for the individual, another for his wife, and another for each dependent. In addition the optional standard deduction, which allows 10% of adjusted gross income up to a total deduction of $1,000, amounts to a further exemption for most taxpayers. However it is an exemption which varies with income.

[228] U.S. Treas. Dep't Study, Individual Income Tax Exemptions (1947); Bastable, Public Finance 317–20 (3d ed., 1922).

[229] But note Taussig's comment: "The demand for the exemption of the lowest tier of incomes results from the same state of mind as the advocacy of progressive taxation. . . ." 2 Taussig, Principles of Economics 499 (1911).

issue between general progression and proportion. At most, under this view, the issue would seem to be merely one of degrees of progression and not one of principle. But the debate can hardly be so illusory, and further analysis shows why a real issue of principle remains.

A flat tax with an exemption—a *degressive* tax[230]—and a tax with graduated marginal rates—a *graduated* tax—are not functional equivalents. Although a degressive tax can always be fully translated into a set of progressive *effective* rates, and although a graduated tax can similarly always be fully translated into a set of progressive *effective* rates, there is no way of stating a given degressive tax by any set of graduated marginal rates, and there is no way of stating a given set of graduated marginal rates as a degressive tax. In other words, the two taxes can never be made equivalent in the sense of affecting all taxpayers under each system alike.

The difference between the two patterns is not a random difference but a systematic one. In the case of a graduated tax it is possible to arrange an infinite variety of patterns of effective rates to raise a given amount of revenue. The striking thing about the progression in a degressive tax is that it always follows the same pattern. Because the progression is due to the exemption, it is possible to state a single mathematical formula which defines the slope of the progression curve in all cases regardless of the amount of the exemption or the level of the flat tax. This is true because the progression results from the fact that the flat rate is applied to only a fraction of the total income and this fraction changes in size as the total income itself changes. Thus, where the total income is twice the amount of the exemption, the effective tax rate is one-half the nominal flat rate; where it is three times, the effective rate is two-thirds; where it is four times, the effective rate is three-fourths, and so on.

From these mathematical propositions several important practical differences between a degressive tax and a graduated tax derive. The most obvious of these is that under a degressive tax the marginal rate of tax is always the same, and is identical with the nominal rate of the tax.[231] For this reason a degressive tax does not have the disadvantageous effects of graduated rates on incentives to work, invest, or save. Under a degressive tax the marginal rate for some taxpayers is higher than it would be under a

[230] The term "degressive" as used here is restricted to the tax curve which results from allowing all taxpayers to deduct the exemption. This is our own usage of the term. It has usually been used to describe any progressive tax curve with decelerating rates or any progressive tax curve which finally reaches a flat rate.

[231] It might be noted that this characteristic of a flat marginal rate is sufficient to indicate why a sacrifice theory premised on declining utility could never be offered as a rationale for such a tax.

graduated tax which raised the same amount of revenue; but the important point here is that the deterrent effect of the degressive tax does not grow as income increases.

A second practical difference, which is a corollary of the flat marginal rate, is that a ceiling in effect is imposed on the marginal rate. Since the marginal rate is constant whatever the level of income, it cannot be increased for those with large incomes without there being an equivalent increase for those just above the exemption level. Consequently, as a practical matter the marginal rate for the wealthy will be set at a level measured by the tolerances of the lower or middle group of taxpayers.

A third practical difference is that much of the uncertainty as to exact rate pattern which has plagued almost all arguments for progression appears to be absent in the case of the degressive tax. As has been shown, there is only one possible curve of progression defined by a degressive tax. And, more significant, once the revenue goal is set only one judgment is required: where to draw the exemption line. Given this judgment, all other questions are automatically answered.

There is another distinguishing characteristic of a degressive curve. In order to raise the same amount of revenue with a milder degree of progression, it can be demonstrated that either some tax would have to be imposed upon those who are below the exemption level, or the marginal rates of tax on those above the exemption level would have to be regressive. Neither of these alternatives is likely to be acceptable. It therefore follows as a practical matter that any pattern of graduated rates which raised the same amount of revenue as a given degressive tax would have to be more progressive. In this sense it can be said that, at a given level of exemption and at a given revenue goal, the degressive tax is the least steep form of progressive tax.

These four differences between degressive and graduated tax structures make it clear why one can grant the case for an exemption and yet consistently reject any graduation. Each of the differences makes the degressive tax more conservative in tendency and operation than any comparable graduated tax. And taken together the points of difference are strongly suggestive of a basic difference in rationale underlying the two types of taxes.[232]

[232] The English scheme of abatements has been virtually a compromise of the two principles. So long as the abatements are rigorously limited it operates about the same as the degressive tax; but as the abatements become more generous the tax becomes explicitly progressive. As noted in text, section 4 supra, the English have constantly experimented with the rates of abatement. It seems reasonably clear that during the nineteenth century the abatements were not regarded as a commitment to progression.

21

So long as a degressive tax is keyed to an exemption set by a rigorously defined minimum level of subsistence, the progression inherent in it, while not negligible, is not very arresting. This probably explains why the literature on progression has had so little concern with the implications of degression.[233]

If in fact the exemption is set by a minimum subsistence standard there is really a further practical difference between the two taxes. The entire rate structure of any degressive tax is dictated, as has been noted, by the single judgment involved in setting the exemption. A judgment about minimum subsistence, although not without its difficulties, is certainly more objective than any of the multiple judgments required to set graduated rates.[234] And even if one is concerned over the possibility of error in setting the subsistence level, the gradualness of the effective rates of a degressive tax for those not far above the exemption is probably sufficient insurance against the error being seriously painful.

It may be difficult however to keep the exemption down at the level of sheer physical survival in our society. Once it starts moving upward toward a "decent standard of living," the dollar significance of the exemption increases and with it the scope of progression.[235] More important, the objectivity of the judgment begins to dissolve and the area of controversy over where to draw the line increases. When this happens, there is but a short step to explicit graduation of rates, at least over a limited area. If it is necessary to compromise conflicting judgments about where to set the exemption, the widest range of possible adjustments is offered by graduation of rates on incomes in the area of controversy. Once such graduation has been introduced to solve the exemption problem the difference between degression and graduation becomes a difference of degree only, and the idea of graduated rates is likely in time to spread throughout the tax structure.

It is possible to move the exemption level out of the context of sub-

[233] The fact that a particular kind of progression is derived from an exemption is frequently noted in the literature. Cohen-Stuart for example refers to it as "Benthamite progression." However it does not appear that anyone has studied the implications of a minimum subsistence exemption with a view to supporting a general theory of progression.

[234] Some of the factors which might be taken into account in setting the minimum subsistence income of a family are its size, the age of its members, and its location within the country. U.S. Treas. Dep't Study, Individual Income Tax Exemptions (1947) is particularly useful in indicating the variations which regional differences might introduce.

[235] There is an extensive treatment by Pigou of the problem of defining the "national minimum standard of real income." Pigou, Economics of Welfare Pt. V, c. XI (1920).

sistence altogether. In theory a degressive tax could be utilized to achieve one of the purposes customarily associated with graduated rates—the redistribution of income in order to lessen economic inequalities. The federal income tax of 1894 with its $4,000 exemption came startlingly close to being this kind of tax. In any event it may be useful to complete the analysis of the case for progression by contrasting such a degressive tax with a comparable graduated tax, and to inquire whether, at this point, the issue between degression and graduation finally becomes trivial.

If the exemption were high the range of the progression from the exemption would be considerable and would be felt by the large majority of taxpayers. The conservative tendencies of degression—the flat marginal rate, the practical ceiling on the marginal rate, the single rate pattern and the single judgment required to set it, and the gentleness of the resulting progression—would all still have significance. But of greater importance here is the fact that such a tax would have the merit of requiring a single, clear-cut distinction on grounds of inequality. The intended beneficiaries of the resulting redistribution would be sharply defined by the distinction between the taxpaying community and the non-taxpaying community. Although the effective rates among taxpayers would vary with income, there would be no ambiguity about the objective of the proposal. In equality terms it would mean that a dividing line had been set; the society in effect would be saying it did not want to reduce by taxes the incomes of any who were below the line, and that it was not concerned with affecting the inequalities in the incomes of those who were above the line. This clarity would give the arrangement the added advantage, or disadvantage, of political candor.

Such clarity in the judgment about equality also suggests that there is a basic ambiguity about the equalitarian objectives of a graduated tax. A degressive tax is basically limited to a comparison of two classes—those below and those above the exemption level. But a graduated tax necessarily involves the comparison of more than two classes. For convenience it can be analyzed by analogy to a comparison of three men: a low income man, a middle income man, and a high income man. Obviously there is inequality between the low income man and the middle and high income men. But there is also inequality between the high income man and the low and middle income men. The crucial point is that one of these inequalities can be mitigated through taxation only at the price of not mitigating so fully through taxation the other inequality. If steps are taken primarily to bring the high income man and the low income man closer, the gap between the middle and the low income men will be less changed than it could have been. Similarly if steps are taken primarily to bring the high and middle incomes closer together, the gap between the middle and the low incomes will remain less changed than it could have been. And finally if steps are taken to reduce the gap between the middle and the low incomes, the gap between the middle and the high incomes will remain less changed.[236] The reason why this ambivalence is peculiar to a graduated tax can be stated generally. Under a degressive tax the progression among taxpayers presumably is simply a by-product and not the purpose of the tax; under a graduated tax designed to lessen economic inequalities the progression presumably is meant to affect not only high and middle incomes relative to low incomes, but also high incomes relative to middle and low incomes.

This ambivalence of graduated rates is not an altogether academic point. It might well be at the heart of the controversy which is going on today over the kind of graduated rate pattern that should be adopted. In this connection it might be useful to think of the "middle class" in our society as being composed of those who are somewhat above the average income level, and the "upper class" as consisting of those who are far above it. Much of the current controversy over the rate pattern concerns the question how, if the progressive rates are to be increased, the lower, middle and upper groups are to share the burden of the increase. It is not obvious which solution would result in a more progressive tax in the sense of one which came closer to bringing about literal equality. Not only is it not obvious, but even if there were knowledge of precisely how many persons had incomes at each level of the income scale, there would still seem to be no basis for choosing between alternative rate patterns. Nor is the difficulty surmounted by deciding whether the proper scale of measurement is in terms of income classes or individuals. As long as there are at least three income classes, the fundamental ambiguity remains, and it is still necessary to decide whether, in stopping short of absolute equality, the objective is to bring the bottom and top closer together, or bring more persons closer to the top, or more persons closer to the bottom.

But this is not the whole story. The degressive tax approach to mitigating inequality has some serious drawbacks of its own. While in theory it is

[236] It is true that a particular set of graduated rates can in part reduce the gap between the top and the bottom men and in part reduce the gap between the middle and bottom. The clearest case of this is where the bottom man is exempted and the other two are taxed in any ratio; both will be brought closer to the low man. But the degree to which the middle man is subject to some tax is a degree to which the gap between the middle man and the top man is not reduced.

The relationships stated remain the same even if the tax money is used to make welfare expenditures for the bottom man. The expenditures operate like an exemption for him.

possible to set the exemption at any level, and then set the single rate of the tax, as a practical matter severe limits are likely to be imposed by the magnitude of the revenue goal. Once the revenue goal is given, the height of the rate is fixed by the height of the exemption. If the revenue goal is relatively large, the price of a high exemption is prohibitively high rates.

Another drawback is that degression would tend to relieve too large a part of the population from the obligation to pay taxes. Whatever the force of democratic participation by way of paying taxes[237] as an argument against having any exemption, it must be recognized that at some point surely there can be too large a number of citizens out from under the tax system. This suggests a rather forceful, and perhaps novel, way of looking at the function of graduated rates. On this view their main function is to permit a wider range for partial exemption from the full rate of tax and thus preserve wider democratic participation in government through paying taxes.[238]

These drawbacks suggest a final difficulty when on equalitarian grounds the exemption is set well above a rigorously defined minimum subsistence level. It may be that on re-examination the advantages of candor and clarity which were thought to inhere in reducing the issue of inequality to a single judgment are, after all, largely illusory. Any line, other than the rigorously defined minimum subsistence line, which attempts to set off those whose unequal position concerns us, is necessarily somewhat arbitrary. Wherever the line is drawn, those who are near but above it will always have a disturbing argument that, in terms of the economic inequalities which exist, their position is more like that of those below them who are exempt from the tax than it is like that of the wealthier above them. The logic of this contention always pushes the exemption one level higher until the tax rests only on the very wealthiest in the community and is at the highest rate practicable. Viewed in this way the drawback of relying on the exemption alone to cope with inequality may be that, while it has the not inconsiderable advantage that it requires only one judgment, it has the disadvantage that the one judgment cannot as a practical matter be made. Once again explicit graduation of rates offers a way of implementing judgments about inequality because it does not rely on a single judgment but admits of a series of less decisive judgments. In this sense graduation is a compromise solution to the inequality issue.

[237] See Bastable, Public Finance 319 (3d ed., 1922).

[238] See Cohn, The Science of Finance 332 (Veblen trans., 1895).

There may then be a dilemma in the effort to get at the problem of economic inequality, at least above a rigorously defined minimum subsistence level. No one seriously proposes to bring everyone in the community to the exact same level of wealth or income. The problem accordingly is one of determining how to lessen inequality short of eliminating it altogether. The most intelligible decision—dividing the community into just two groups—is the least practicable, and the most feasible decision—to graduate the community into many groups—is the least clear.

From these observations and speculations about degression some further conclusions about progression in general are available. The difference between degression and graduated rates remains in the end one of principle, although it is a subtle difference. The proposal of either radically high or radically low exemptions will almost certainly invite the compromise proposal to graduate rates to some degree. If the exemption is of those below the subsistence minimum, graduation will be required to soften the impact of the tax on the poor. If the exemption is set high on equality grounds, both fiscal and political considerations will again call for graduated rates to keep enough persons in the system as taxpayers. Finally, these considerations invite a suspicion, albeit rather faint, that the whole elaborate superstructure of graduated rates is but a by-product of the difficulties of handling the exemption problem.

22

It may be fitting to approach the conclusion of this study of the case for progression by looking once again explicitly at the relevance of government expenditures. At an early point in the discussion, in connection with the examination of benefit theory, direct attention was paid to the significance of expenditures. After that point the discussion proceeded on the express assumption that the allocation of the tax burden could be analyzed apart from the pattern of expenditures by the government. Now it is proper to consider whether this basic assumption has in any way distorted the analysis and to ascertain whether any additional insights about progression can be gained by reflecting upon expenditures.

In classifying government expenditures for present purposes it is convenient to make two distinctions. There are expenditures the benefits of which are directly traceable to particular individuals and there are those the benefits of which are diffusely distributed throughout the community. Among the traceable expenditures there are those which are intended as "subsidies" to the recipients and there are those which are not intended as subsidies. These two distinctions result in three general types of expenditures: those which are traceable but are not intended as subsidies, those which are not traceable, and those which are traceable and are intended as subsidies.

The first type raises no new questions. Almost by definition such expenditures call for application of the benefit principle for distributing the tax burden created by them. Particular individuals are receiving economic benefits from the government under circumstances in which there is no intention to enrich them. Unless the beneficiaries are required to pay for the value of goods or services they receive, the expenditures would operate to bestow unintended subsidies on them, and thus to redistribute wealth or income.

Expenditures of the second type—those the benefits of which are not traceable—are more complex to analyze. It will be recalled that the existence of this category of expenditures has traditionally provided a decisive argument against wider use of the benefit principle. If the benefits of the expenditures of government cannot be traced directly, the tax burden corresponding to such expenditures cannot be allocated by application of the usual benefit criterion. The traditional way of proceeding analytically has been simply to ignore the expenditure side altogether and to assume that none of those who pay the taxes covering these expenditures receive any offsetting economic benefits. In effect this results in treating the collection of taxes as though it were only a common disaster—as though the tax money once collected were thrown into the sea. It is from this perspective that much of sacrifice theory derives its original appeal, for the tax problem can then be stated as one of apportioning the burdens of the common disaster. Implicit in the notion that the disaster ought to be borne equally is the judgment that it ought not be the occasion for changing relatively the real economic position of the parties.

Except perhaps on the unkindest view of the good sense of government expenditures, it is of course a fiction to treat them as though they produced no offsetting benefits. But like many fictions in law this fiction is a shorthand way of making sense. In general, if one must act and if the result of acting depends on at least two variables, one of which cannot be known within the time for action, the most reasonable course is not to act blindly but to act on the basis of the known variable only. In the present context this means that since we cannot trace the benefits flowing from the expenditures we should act on the basis of the knowledge we have—knowledge of the consequences of the collection of the tax alone. It thus is rational to use either sacrifice or economic equality criteria for the collection of taxes even though the expenditures may be producing, in an unknown way, offsetting benefits and thus defeating what we think we are doing.

If this approach through ignorance is not appealing there is another way of looking at the matter which leads to the same conclusion. Although admittedly many expenditures of government cannot be traced directly, there is, as was suggested in the discussion of benefit theory, some plausibility to the assumption that all citizens benefit equally from such expenditures. The clearest instance is that of military expenditures for exterior security. Here the life and freedom of everyone in the community are equally at stake, and in this sense everybody equally benefits from the protection. In modern times virtually no one has been willing to follow up this clue as to benefits. The reason seems to be that the resulting tax would be regressive with income. The benefits of military protection, and other vital services of government, in no way put money or its equivalent in the taxpayer's pocket. The only perceptible economic consequence of the tax and the expenditure would lie in the taking of equal sums from all taxpayers and thus in redistributing income in the direction of greater inequality. Whether or not a case for increasing inequality ever could be made, it certainly is intolerable to predicate it on the cost of the indispensable activities of government.

From this review it is seen that the case for progression is neither strengthened nor weakened by taking the first two categories of expenditures into account; and further, that in ignoring such expenditures the prior analysis of the merits of progression was not distorted.

It is the third category of expenditures, those intended as subsidies— and here we are concerned only with welfare subsidies to those with small incomes—that has most often been tied to the case for progressive taxation.[239] If the society is to make welfare payments, so the argument runs, must it not, to be consistent, collect the taxes to cover such payments on a progressive basis? Before turning to this question, it is important to distinguish and to put aside one class of expenditures which, although not intended as subsidies, are frequently lumped together with subsidies as welfare expenditures. Any expenditures which operate on the insurance principle may furnish an example. It may be desirable that all members of the community be insured against accidents, ill health, and the like. If the state elects to provide the compulsory insurance directly, it might decide

---

[239] Such welfare payments, especially if made in cash, can be viewed as an extension of the income tax below the exemption level, and hence as a "negative" income tax.

to collect the premiums in the form of taxes. But this by itself does not indicate what the pattern of such taxation ought to be. It could well be a sufficient welfare goal of the state to compel this much prudent "sumptuary expenditure" by its citizens without at the same time seeking to redistribute wealth or income. While this distinction between redistribution and sumptuary expenditures may be of crucial importance in analyzing the nature and merits of given welfare proposals, it need not concern us further. If only sumptuary expenditures and not redistributive objectives are involved, they would seem to be proper occasions for taxing according to the benefit principle.

But even the true welfare subsidy presents no new arguments for, or against, progression. If one has decided that the cost of the general nontraceable expenditures of government should be borne progressively, the reasons supporting that decision necessarily would apply with at least equal force to apportioning the cost of welfare subsidy expenditures. Conversely, if one has decided that such general expenditures should be borne proportionately, there is no impetus to reach a different conclusion as to the welfare payments. Where the payments are confined to those below the minimum subsistence level they are simply a means of implementing the judgment about the exemption itself. The cost of these payments stands on the same footing, from the point of view of allocating it among taxpayers, as the "cost" of the exemption. Thus whatever argument there may be about apportioning the burden of the welfare payments, it can only mirror arguments already met in the discussion of the exemption. Essentially the same analysis would apply where the exemption is set well above the subsistence level and specifically for the sake of redressing economic inequalities.

In no case, then, need the nature of the expenditure affect the debate as to how the tax burden should be distributed. But it may be well to note that the character of the tax system may affect the nature and the magnitude of the expenditures. The appearance of substantial welfare expenditures has almost paralleled the rise of progressive taxation. It is not improbable that, as a political matter, some of the expenditures would not have been undertaken were it not for progression.

23

The case for progression, after a long critical look, thus turns out to be stubborn but uneasy. The most distinctive and technical arguments advanced in its behalf are the weakest. It is hard to gain much comfort from the special arguments, however intricate their formulations, constructed on notions of benefit, sacrifice, ability to pay, or economic stability. The case has stronger appeal when progressive taxation is viewed as a means of reducing economic inequalities. But the case for more economic equality, when examined directly, is itself perplexing. And the perplexity is greatly magnified for those who in the quest for greater equality are unwilling to argue for radical changes in the fundamental institutions of the society.

These implications apart, the theory of progression is a matter of major importance for taxation. The adoption of progression necessarily influences the positive law of taxation more than any other factor. But in the end it is the implications about economic inequality which impart significance and permanence to the issue and institution of progression. Ultimately a serious interest in progression stems from the fact that a progressive tax is perhaps the cardinal instance of the democratic community struggling with its hardest problem.

APPENDIX

Following its publication in book form in 1953, *The Uneasy Case* was widely reviewed. Some of the major reviews may be of interest as contemporary commentary on the progression issue.

WILLIAM H. ANDERSON, 27 So. Cal. L. Rev. 502 (1954)
ROY BLOUGH, 56 Col. L. Rev. 809 (1956)
JOHN CHAMBERLAIN, 21 Chi. L. Rev. 502 (1954)
LEO A. DIAMOND, 8 Rutgers L. Rev. 556 (1954)
LOUIS EISENSTEIN, 9 Reading Guide 36 (1954)
HAROLD M. GROVES, 291 Annals 176 (1954)
F. A. HAYEK, 4 The Freeman 229 (1953)
JOHN JEWKES, 7 Nat'l Tax J. 377 (1954)
M. SLADE KENDRICK, 39 Cornell L. Q. 370 (1954)
ROBERT KRAMER, 44 Virg. L. Rev. 379 (1958)
R. MAGILL, 40 A. B. A. J. 51 (1954)
HENRY G. MANNE, Taxes 79 (Jan. 1954)
DONALD J. MAY, 2 J. Pub. L. 429 (Fall 1953)
RANDOLPH PAUL, 67 Harv. L. Rev. 725 (1954)
JEWELL J. RASMUSSEN, 4 Utah L. Rev. 152 (1954)
NORMAN REDLICH, 7 J. Legal Ed. 450 (1955)
LEWIS E. WAGNER, 39 Iowa L. Rev. 525 (1954)
HASKELL WALD, 65 Ethics 68 (1954)
DAVID McCORD WRIGHT, 6 Stan. L. Rev. 583 (1954)

TOPICAL INDEX

NAME INDEX

PHOENIX BOOKS
in Political Science and Law